PACEMAKER®

Basic
English

Third Edition

WORKBOOK

GLOBE FEARON

Pearson Learning Group

REVIEWERS
We thank the following educators, who provided valuable comments
and suggestions during the development of this book:

Patricia Berdan, Will Rogers Middle School, Fair Oaks, California
Nina Berler, William Annin Middle School, Basking Ridge, New Jersey
Dr. Dennis J. Carroll, Susan Wagner High School, Staten Island, New York
Carol Donahue, Neptune Middle School, Neptune, New Jersey
Christie Dorn, Indio High School, Indio, California
Ann Hilborn, Lee High School, Houston, Texas
Stephani Jones, Farmingdale High School, Farmingdale, New York
Barbara Loga, Bellevue High School, Bellevue, Michigan
Patsy Mills, Bellaire High School, Bellaire, Texas
Mary Moore, Frost Curriculum Center, Warren, Michigan
Anika Simmons, North Star Academy Charter School, Newark, New Jersey
Mildred Teague, Wallkill Valley Regional High School, Hamburg, New Jersey

Subject Area Consultant: Paul Gallaher, Florida Department of Education- Bureau of Instructional
Support and Community Services, Tallahassee, Florida, Marcia Krefetz-Levine, Brookdale Community
College, Lincroft, New Jersey, Paula Young, Orange County Public Schools, Orlando, Florida
Pacemaker Curriculum Advisor: Stephen C. Larsen, formerly of The University of Texas at Austin

Executive Editor: Eleanor Ripp
Senior Editor: Karen McCollum
Editor: Ayanna Taylor
Editorial Developer: Pinnacle Education Associates
Production Editor: Travis Bailey
Designers: Susan Brorein, Jennifer Visco, Evelyn Bauer
Editorial Assistants: Amy Greenberg, Kathy Bentzen, Wanda Rockwell
Market Manager: Katie Kehoe-Erezuma
Research Director: Angela Darchi
Electronic Composition: Burmar Technical Corp., Phyllis Rosinsky, Linda Bierniak

About the Cover: English skills help people communicate effectively with one another. The images
on the cover of this book show how an understanding of basic English skills is relevant in everyday
life. People read books for enjoyment and to gather information. Newspapers tell about current
events. Telephones allow people to speak and listen to one another. Dictionaries give definitions,
correct spelling, and pronunciation of words. Computers can be used to write personal letters and
reports for school. How do you use English skills in your everyday life?

ISBN 0-130-23314-5
Printed in the United States of America
8 9 10 11   05

1-800-321-3106
www.pearsonlearning.com

Contents

A Note to the Student

Use this workbook along with your *Pacemaker Basic English* textbook. Each exercise in the workbook is linked to a lesson in your textbook. This workbook will help you do three things—review, practice, and think critically.

Each exercise starts with a quick **review** to remind you of the basic English skills and concepts from the lesson. This boxed review will help you complete the practice exercises that follow. You can use this boxed review as a study tool. Use it whenever you want to review a skill. It will help you to remember what you have learned.

Practice in the skills and concepts of the lesson follow the boxed review. The more you practice, the more you will remember. Set goals for yourself, and try to meet them as you do each set of exercises. Practice helps you master skills and leads to success on tests, in school, at work, and in life.

Your **critical thinking** skills are challenged when you do the activities at the bottom of the page. Critical thinking means putting information to use. For example, you may review and practice how to capitalize proper nouns. Then you may have to use this information to write a sentence about your favorite book or magazine. That is, you will apply what you know to a different situation. This is critical thinking!

Your textbook is a wonderful source of knowledge. By studying it, you will learn a great deal about basic English. The real value of this information will come when you have mastered these skills and put critical thinking to use.

▶1.1 What Is a Sentence?   Exercise 1

> A **sentence** is a group of words that expresses a complete thought. Every sentence has a **subject** and a **predicate**. The subject tells who or what the sentence is about. The predicate tells what the subject does or is. A **fragment** is a group of words that does not express a complete thought. In the sentence below, the subject is underlined once. The predicate is underlined twice.
>
> Sentence: The game starts in ten minutes.
> Fragment: The coach of this team.

**Look at each group of words. Write *sentence* for each sentence.
Write *fragment* for each fragment.**

1. The concert is tomorrow night. _____

2. Many different bands will play. _____

3. To hear my favorite group. _____

4. I bought tickets last week. _____

5. My friend Brian. _____

6. We like the same kind of music. _____

7. The first band plays at seven o'clock. _____

8. Want to get there early. _____

9. The concert hall downtown. _____

10. It will be a great show! _____

CRITICAL THINKING

**The following group of words is a fragment. Tell what part is
missing–*subject* or *predicate*. Then write the fragment as a
complete sentence.**

My favorite kind of music _____

_____

Name _____   Date _____

▶ 1.2 Kinds of Sentences   Exercise 2

A **declarative sentence** tells what someone or something is or does.
An **interrogative sentence** asks a question.
An **imperative sentence** gives a command or makes a request.
An **exclamatory sentence** shows strong feeling.

Declarative:	I like to read mysteries.
Interrogative:	Does the library have any new mystery books?
Imperative:	Look on the bookshelf.
Exclamatory:	Here is one from my favorite author!

Label each sentence. Write *declarative, interrogative, imperative,*
or *exclamatory*.

1. When does Eric's plane arrive? _____

2. It should be here in ten minutes. _____

3. This airport is so crowded! _____

4. Please check that this is the correct gate. _____

CRITICAL THINKING

Choose one of the following words: *concert, shopping, laugh.*
Write a declarative, interrogative, imperative, and exclamatory
sentence using the word you chose.

1. Declarative: _____

_____

2. Interrogative: _____

_____

3. Imperative: _____

_____

4. Exclamatory: _____

_____

2   Chapter 1 • Sentences

Name _____ Date _____

 1.3 Capital Letters and End Punctuation in Sentences   **Exercise 3**

A sentence begins with a capital letter and ends with a punctuation mark. A declarative sentence ends with a period. An interrogative sentence ends with a question mark. An imperative sentence ends with a period or an exclamation point. An exclamatory sentence ends with an exclamation point.

Declarative: This box is heavy.	Interrogative: Is this the box?
Imperative: Open it and see.	Exclamatory: This is great!

Rewrite each sentence below. Use capital letters and end punctuation correctly.

1. what do you like on your pizza _____

_____

2. pepperoni pizza is my favorite _____

_____

3. order a large pizza for us _____

_____

4. did you order drinks too _____

_____

5. this pizza tastes great _____

_____

CRITICAL THINKING

When would you use an exclamation point at the end of an imperative sentence? _____

_____

1.4 Subjects and Predicates in Declarative Sentences

In most declarative sentences, the subject comes before the predicate. In some declarative sentences, the predicate comes before the subject. In the examples below, the subject is underlined once. The predicate is underlined twice.

Alice tripped on something. (subject before the predicate)

On the ground were two rocks. (subject after the predicate)

For each sentence, draw one line under the subject. Draw two lines under the predicate.

1. Daniel's room looks very neat.

2. The bed is made nicely.

3. On top of the bed are three large pillows.

4. All of his clothes are folded neatly in the drawers.

5. His books are stacked on the bookshelves.

6. On one shelf sit all of his trophies.

7. A bulletin board holds pictures of his friends.

8. All of his shoes are put away in the closet.

9. On one wall hangs a poster of his favorite hockey team.

10. Daniel works hard to keep his room clean.

CRITICAL THINKING

Read each group of words below. Decide whether the subject or the predicate is missing. Write the answer on the line.

1. An alarm clock. _____

2. Washed the windows. _____

Name _____ Date _____

1.5 Subjects and Predicates in Interrogative Sentences

In some interrogative sentences, part of the predicate comes before the subject. To find the subject, change the sentence into a declarative sentence. Then look for the subject near the beginning of the sentence. In the second example below, the subject is underlined once. The predicate is underlined twice.

Interrogative: Can you fix my computer?
Declarative: You can fix my computer.

Rewrite each interrogative sentence as a declarative sentence. Draw one line under the subject. Draw two lines under the predicate.

1. Has Suzanne sent you an e-mail message today? _____

_____

2. Does she know my e-mail address? _____

_____

3. Is the message about our meeting tomorrow? _____

_____

4. Will you print a copy of the message for me? _____

_____

CRITICAL THINKING

How can changing an interrogative sentence to a declarative sentence help you find the subject and predicate?

_____

_____

_____

1.6 Subjects and Predicates in Imperative Sentences

Exercise 6

In most imperative sentences, only the predicate is written or spoken. The subject of the sentence is understood to be there. This understood subject is always *you*.

Open the window. (The subject is understood: *you*)

Write the subject of each sentence below. Some of the sentences are imperative sentences. If the subject is understood to be *you*, write *you*.

1. We need to get ready for tonight's party. _____

2. Blow up all of the balloons. _____

3. Tie balloons to each of the chairs. _____

4. The streamers should be hung from the ceiling. _____

5. Watch out for the ceiling fan! _____

6. This banner should go on that wall. _____

7. Set these plates on the table. _____

8. Be careful! _____

9. When will the food be ready? _____

10. Make sure we have enough ice. _____

CRITICAL THINKING

The following sentence is an interrogative sentence. Rewrite it as an imperative sentence.

Would you hold these books? _____

_____

Name _____   Date _____

 1.7 Writing Complete Sentences   **Exercise 7**

> A complete sentence has a subject and a predicate. It begins with
> a capital letter and ends with a punctuation mark.
>
> Follow the READ, PLAN, WRITE, and CHECK steps to write complete
> sentences. The questions below will help you CHECK your writing.
>
> **CHECK How can you improve your writing?**
> - Does your sentence answer the assignment?
> - Did you use subjects and predicates correctly?
> - How can you make your writing clearer?

Complete the writing assignments below.

1. Write a sentence that tells about a kind thing someone did
for you. Explain who it was and what this person did.

_____

_____

_____

2. Write a sentence that tells about a kind thing you did for
someone. Tell what you did and for whom you did it.

_____

_____

_____

PUTTING IT ALL TOGETHER

How can people show kindness to others? On a separate sheet of
paper, write a paragraph about kind things people can do for one
another. You may want to use the sentences you have written
above. Add other sentences to explain your ideas.

2.1 Using Commas to Avoid Confusion in a Sentence

A **comma** is used to show a short break or pause between words. You can use commas to make your writing easier to understand.

Incorrect:	When I get home I must study for my test.
Correct:	When I get home, I must study for my test.

Write each sentence. Use a comma where it is needed to make the sentence easier to understand.

1. Late last night something woke me up.

_____

2. As I sat up in bed I looked around the room.

_____

3. Then outside my window I saw a bright flash of light.

_____

4. After a few minutes I heard the loud thunder.

_____

5. Before long the rain was falling hard.

_____

CRITICAL THINKING

Read the following sentence aloud. Explain how you can tell where a comma is needed. Then write the sentence correctly.

Since it was late and I was very tired I went straight to bed.

_____

_____

_____

Name _____   Date _____

 2.2 Using Commas to Set Off Words
in a Sentence   **Exercise 9**

Use a comma to separate introductory words from the rest of a sentence. Use a comma to set off words that interrupt the flow of thought in a sentence. When a person is called by name in a sentence, use a comma to separate that person's name from the rest of the sentence.

After the race, I was tired. (introductory words)
Collin is, in fact, the winner. (interrupting words)
Helen, did you see him win? (person's name)

Write each sentence. Use commas as needed to set off a word or group of words from the rest of the sentence.

1. Emilio do you remember where we parked the car?

_____

2. This I think is the right row.

_____

3. Well I don't see the car anywhere.

_____

4. It is I hope behind that big truck.

_____

5. There it is Susan.

_____

CRITICAL THINKING

Add an introductory word or group of words to the sentence below. Punctuate the sentence correctly.

We can leave soon. _____

_____

▶ 2.3 Using Commas in a Series   Exercise 10

A series is a list of three or more items in a row within a sentence.
Use a comma between each item in a series.

Elaine asked Marla, Ted, and Shawn to help her.
This machine takes nickels, dimes, and quarters.
He stopped his bike, stepped off, and chained it to the gate.

Add commas to the sentences below to separate the items in a series.

1. Our school colors are gold red and blue.

2. The gym cafeteria and auditorium are on the first floor.

3. Books pens and papers all lay neatly on the desk.

4. Mr. Sims takes attendance gives tests and checks our work.

5. I brought a sandwich potato chips and an apple for lunch.

6. We played soccer basketball and tennis before lunch.

7. After lunch, I have English history science and math.

8. I tutor on Monday Wednesday and Friday.

9. Today, I took a test read a book and finished my science project.

10. Mrs. Keane told us about Paris London Rome and Madrid.

CRITICAL THINKING

Complete the following sentences. Include a series in each sentence.

1. Yesterday, I _____.

2. The wrapping paper was _____.

3. The cars were _____.

Name _____ Date _____

2.4 Using Commas in Dates   **Exercise 11**

> When you write a date, use a comma to separate the day of the
> month from the year. If the sentence continues after the date, put a
> comma after the year. A date that has only the month and the year
> does not need a comma.
>
> My brother was born on April 30, 1987.
> January 25, 1990, was the day my sister was born.
> We moved here in March 1995.

**Write each sentence. Add commas to the dates as needed. If the
sentence is correct, write *correct*.**

1. The first U.S. satellite was sent into space on January 31 1958.

_____

2. Weather pictures were sent from a satellite in April 1960.

_____

3. The first satellite to use nuclear power was sent into orbit on June 29 1961.

_____

4. Canada's first satellite went into space in September 1962 .

_____

5. A satellite was sent into orbit on April 2 1963 to study the atmosphere.

_____

CRITICAL THINKING

**Write a sentence about something you remember from your
childhood. Include the date. Use commas as needed.**

_____

_____

_____

▶ 2.4 Using Commas in Place Names   Exercise 12

> When you write place names, use a comma to separate the city and
> the state or country. If the sentence continues after a place name,
> use a comma after the state or country.
>
> My dad once flew to Rome, Italy.
> I lived in Erie, Pennsylvania, for only one year.

**Write each sentence. Add commas to the place names
as needed.**

1. Boston Massachusetts has a large public library.

_____

2. Tucson Arizona is a popular vacation spot.

_____

3. Virginia Beach Virginia has a very busy harbor.

_____

4. Someone once compared Venice Italy to Seattle Washington.

_____

5. Toledo Ohio is farther north than Toledo Spain.

_____

CRITICAL THINKING

Write one sentence about a place you have seen or would
like to go. Include the name of the city and state or country.
Use commas as needed.

_____

_____

_____

2.5 Using Commas or Exclamation Points with Interjections

> An **interjection** is a word or group of words that expresses emotion. Use a comma after an interjection at the beginning of a sentence. Use an exclamation point if the interjection shows strong emotion. Capitalize the first word after the exclamation point.
>
> Hey, does anyone know where my notebook is?
> Hey! Don't step on that broken glass.

Write each sentence. Punctuate each interjection. Use either a comma or an exclamation point.

1. Oh I hope it's not cloudy tonight.

_____

2. Wow Did you see that shooting star?

_____

3. Yes I hope we see some more.

_____

4. Well let's sit here and wait for another one.

_____

5. Ouch I stepped on something.

_____

CRITICAL THINKING

How do you know whether to use a comma or an exclamation point after an interjection?

_____

_____

▶ 2.6 Punctuating Direct Quotations   Exercise 14

Use **quotation marks** at the beginning and end of a direct quotation. Use a comma to separate the quotation from the words that tell who is speaking. At the end of a sentence, place a period inside the quotation marks. Place other punctuation inside the quotation marks if it belongs to the quotation.

"The guests should be arriving any time," said Michael.
Angela said, "Please answer the door."
"Sheila's here!" called Michael. "Hooray!"

Write each sentence. Add quotation marks, commas, and the correct end punctuation where they are needed.

1. This bus is always late said Jenna.

_____

2. Would you like to walk asked her mother.

_____

3. No way Jenna answered. We can wait.

_____

4. Her mother said I guess you are right.

_____

5. Jenna smiled and said Here comes the bus now!

_____

CRITICAL THINKING

The sentence below has two mistakes in punctuation. Write the sentence correctly. Explain why you made these corrections.

The woman asked; "Where does this bus go"? _____

_____

Name _____ Date _____

 2.6 Capitalizing Direct Quotations **Exercise 15**

> The first word of a direct quotation begins with a capital letter.
> Sometimes, a quotation is split into two parts. If the second part of
> the quotation is part of the sentence, do not begin that part with a
> capital letter. If the second part of the quotation is a new sentence,
> use a capital letter.
>
> "Hart Street is blocked off," said the police officer.
> "When do you think," asked the woman, "it will be open?"
> "I am not sure," he answered. "It may be open tomorrow."

**Write each sentence correctly. Use capital letters where they
are needed.**

1. "our fruit market," he said proudly, "is 50 years old."

   _____

2. Lou asked, "did your father start the business?"

   _____

3. "no," answered Mr. Lee, "it was my grandfather."

   _____

4. "how did he get started?" asked Lou.

   _____

5. "his cousin had a farm," Mr. Lee said. "granddad bought fruit there."

   _____

CRITICAL THINKING

**Change the indirect quotation below into a direct quotation.
Use correct capitalization and punctuation.**

Tony said that he was offered a new job. _____

_____

▶ 2.7 Using Colons   Exercise 16

> Use a **colon** to introduce a series of items. When you write an
> expression of time with numerals, use a colon between the hour
> and the minutes. Use a colon after the greeting in a business letter.
>
> The following members spoke: Dale, Amy, and Tina. (series)
> The meeting began at 7:15 P.M. (time)
> Dear Dr. Perry: (greeting)

**Write each fragment or sentence. Use a colon where
it is needed.**

1. Dear Mr. Hamilton

_____

2. He went to the following places the mall, the park, and the fair.

_____

3. We have to leave by 1230, or we'll be late for the show.

_____

4. We packed the following things water, snacks, and a camera.

_____

5. Tim has to fly to the following cities Dallas, Miami, and San Jose.

_____

CRITICAL THINKING

**Write one sentence listing some of the things you see in your
classroom. Use a colon in your sentence.**

_____

_____

_____

2.7 Using Semicolons

Exercise 17

> A **semicolon** joins two closely related sentences into one sentence. After the semicolon, do not use the words *and*, *but*, or *so*. Do not capitalize the word after the semicolon.
>
> The wall seemed bare; we hung a picture.

Write each sentence using a semicolon. Remember to take out any words you no longer need.

1. We are going to move soon, but we do not know where yet.

_____

2. Joe knows of some nice apartments they are on the East Side.

_____

3. The first building was too far away, so we had to keep looking.

_____

4. We did not like the next apartment, and it was too small.

_____

5. We went home, but we will look tomorrow.

_____

CRITICAL THINKING

Read the following sentence. Tell why a semicolon should *not* be used to join the two sentences.

Let's eat lunch; the sun is too bright.

_____

_____

_____

Name _____   Date _____

▶ 2.7 Using Hyphens   **Exercise 18**

Use a **hyphen** to write compound numbers from twenty-one
through ninety-nine. Use a hyphen in a fraction that describes
another word. Use a hyphen in certain compound words.

    seventy-four, eighty-eight (numbers)
    one-third, two-fifths (fractions)
    cross-country, great-grandfather (compound words)

**Write the compound number or fraction in the sentences
below. Use hyphens correctly.**

1. We have driven forty five miles. _____

2. Our gas tank is two thirds full. _____

3. Chicago is still twenty three miles away. _____

4. The price is now one half lower. _____

Complete each sentence with a compound word from the box.

one-way	great-grandmother	play-off	tune-up

5. My _____ was born long ago in Italy.

6. I took my car to the auto shop to get a _____.

7. This is a _____ street.

8. The first _____ game for our team is tonight.

CRITICAL THINKING
Write one sentence that uses two hyphenated words.

_____

_____

_____

Name _____ Date _____

Correct punctuation makes it easy for readers to understand your writing. Remember that a comma separates each item in a series.

Follow the READ, PLAN, WRITE, and CHECK steps to write sentences with correct punctuation. The questions below will help you CHECK your writing.

CHECK **How can you improve your writing?**

- Does your sentence answer the assignment?
- Did you use punctuation correctly?
- How can you make your writing clearer?

Complete the writing assignments below.

1. Write a sentence that lists three things that make you smile. Use commas correctly.

_____

_____

_____

2. Write a sentence that lists three people who make you laugh. Use commas correctly.

_____

_____

_____

PUTTING IT ALL TOGETHER

What kinds of things make you happy? On a separate sheet of paper, write a paragraph about things that make you smile or laugh. You may want to use the sentences you have written above. Add other sentences to explain your ideas.

3.1 What Is a Noun?   Exercise 20

A **noun** names a person, place, thing, event, or idea.

Person	Place	Thing	Event	Idea
boss	store	desk	meeting	liberty
Mrs. Mills	New York	airplane	wedding	courage

Write the nouns in each sentence. There is more than one noun in each sentence.

1. Mount Everest is the highest mountain in the world.

_____

2. The whole mountain is covered with snow except the peaks.

_____

3. Almost no life is found on Mount Everest.

_____

4. Only spiders and insects have been found at the higher levels.

_____

5. Many people have climbed to the top.

_____

CRITICAL THINKING

Fill in the chart with nouns of your own.

Person	Place	Thing	Event	Idea

▶ 3.2 Compound Nouns   Exercise 21

> A **compound noun** is a group of words that names a person, place, thing, event, or idea. Some compound nouns have hyphens between the words. Some are written as one word. Others are a group of words.
>
> half-dollar, sister-in-law (with hyphens)
> toothache, crosswalk (one word)
> post office, Kentucky Derby (group of words)

Write the nouns in each sentence. Then underline the compound nouns.

1. Go down the highway to Ferris Street.

_____

2. At the riverfront, stop at the last streetlight.

_____

3. You will see a steamboat near the docks.

_____

4. In the boathouse, you will see a picture.

_____

5. The man in the picture is your great-grandfather.

_____

CRITICAL THINKING

Use the following words to make as many compound nouns as you can: *day, out, time, light, house, dream.*

_____

_____

Name_____ Date_____

▶ 3.3 Common and Proper Nouns

A **common noun** names any person, place, thing, event, or idea.
A **proper noun** names a certain person, place, thing, event, or idea.
All important words in a proper noun are capitalized.

	Common Noun	Proper Noun
Person	woman	Megan Hale
Place	city	Miami
Thing	month	March
Event	race	Tri-City Motor Race
Idea	religion	Taoism

Write the proper nouns in each sentence.

1. Lucy had a party at the Waterford Inn. _____

2. She hired a band named The Fifth-Street Players. _____

3. Nate, her cousin from Boston, was at the party. _____

4. Lucy ordered food from the Midtown Café. _____

5. Nate gave her tickets to a show in Baltimore. _____

6. Since it was August, the party was outdoors. _____

CRITICAL THINKING

**Rewrite the sentences below. Replace the underlined words
with proper nouns.**

1. My friend used to live in that city.

_____

2. That athlete plays for this team.

_____

▶ 3.4 Capitalizing Names of Places and Parts of the Country   Exercise 23

> The names of places are proper nouns. Names of parts of the United States are also proper nouns. Capitalize the names of regions, or parts, of the country. Do not capitalize names of directions.
>
> The <u>Southwest</u> is the driest part of the country. (region)
> The birds flew <u>south</u> for the winter. (direction)

Rewrite each sentence. Capitalize the proper nouns.

1. Early settlers from england lived in the northeast.

   _____

2. Many settlers from spain lived in the southeast.

   _____

3. Traveling north meant crossing the great smoky mountains.

   _____

4. As people moved west, they crossed the ohio river.

   _____

5. From tennessee, some people traveled northwest to iowa.

   _____

CRITICAL THINKING

**The sentence below has some mistakes in capitalization.
Write it correctly. Explain why you made those corrections.**

We drove South to florida before traveling to the southwest.

_____

_____

3.4 Capitalizing Abbreviations

An **abbreviation** is a shortened form of a word. Sometimes, proper nouns are shortened. Capitalize the first letter of the abbreviations of proper nouns. Put a period at the end. Capitalize both letters in abbreviations of states in the United States. Do not put a period at the end.

Noun	Abbreviation
Mister	Mr.
Avenue	Ave.
Florida	FL

Rewrite each address correctly. Use capital letters and periods if they are needed. Underline the abbreviations.

1. miss allison musgrave
   758 picket ln
   cornelius, nc 28031

   _____

   _____

   _____

2. mr keith nash
   4329 white swan ct
   maple grove, mn 55369

   _____

   _____

   _____

CRITICAL THINKING

Write the address of your school on the envelope below.

J.J. Summers
One Eastway Road
New Town, ST 02000

_____

_____

_____

3.4 Capitalizing Titles   Exercise 25

> Titles of books, movies, magazines, games, and television programs
> are proper nouns. Capitalize the important words in titles. Short
> words such as *and*, *the*, and *of* are not important. In a title, the first
> and last words are always capitalized.
>
> I want to read the book called *Around the World in 80 Days*.
> *Gone With the Wind* is one of my favorite movies.

Capitalize the title in each sentence correctly.

1. When was the movie *the wizard of oz* made?

_____

2. I just finished reading the book *island of the blue dolphins*.

_____

3. The next book I read will be *call of the wild*.

_____

4. I like to watch the television show *life in the big city*.

_____

5. Have you seen my *sports monthly* magazine?

_____

6. There are many interesting facts in *the world almanac*.

_____

CRITICAL THINKING

Write a sentence about a book or magazine you have read.
Capitalize the title of the book or magazine.

_____

_____

Name _____ Date _____

3.5 Writing: Using Nouns in Sentences

Exercise 26

> We use many common and proper nouns when we write sentences.
>
> Follow the READ, PLAN, WRITE, and CHECK steps to write sentences with common and proper nouns. The tips below will help you PLAN your writing.
>
> **PLAN** **Gather your ideas and organize them.**
> - Read the assignment and discuss your ideas with a partner.
> - Use a topic web to organize your ideas.

Complete the writing assignments below.

1. You just found a buried treasure chest. Write a sentence telling how and where you found it. Use at least one proper noun.

_____

_____

_____

2. You open the treasure chest to see what is inside. Write a sentence telling what you see. Use at least one common noun.

_____

_____

_____

PUTTING IT ALL TOGETHER

What is exciting about finding new things? On a separate sheet of paper, write a paragraph about a treasure chest you found. Tell how and where you found it, what you have found, and what you will do with it. You may want to use the sentences you have written above. Add other sentences to explain what you will do with the treasure chest.

> A **singular noun** names one person, place, thing, event, or idea. A **plural noun** names more than one person, place, thing, event, or idea. Many plural nouns end in -*s*.
>
> | Singular Noun | Plural Noun |
> | --- | --- |
> | stream | streams |
> | Lake Superior | the Great Lakes |

Write the nouns in each sentence. If a noun is singular, write *S* after it. If a noun is plural, write *P* after it.

1. Joe and Nick decided to go on a hiking trip.

_____

2. The teens packed a tent, sleeping bags, and extra blankets.

_____

3. Nick studied maps and planned the route.

_____

4. Joe and Nick hiked for eight miles the first day.

_____

5. Joe saw a hawk, a squirrel, and three rabbits.

_____

CRITICAL THINKING

Look around you. List three singular nouns and three plural nouns that you see.

Singular Nouns: _____

Plural Nouns: _____

▶ 4.1 Identifying Collective Nouns   Exercise 28

A **collective noun** names a group of people, things, or animals that act as one unit. Some collective nouns are in the box below.

Collective Nouns				
audience	band	club	committee	crew
crowd	group	pack	squad	swarm

Write the collective noun in each sentence.

1. Mrs. Nash's class is studying animals. _____

2. They study animals that live in a group. _____

3. A herd of elephants lives together. _____

4. Wolves and wild dogs live in a pack. _____

5. A swarm of bees sometimes attacks other animals. _____

6. A flock of geese flies long distances. _____

7. A committee of teachers will judge the reports. _____

8. A crowd gathers to see the winner. _____

CRITICAL THINKING

Each noun on the left is a collective noun. Decide which thing or animal on the right makes up that collective noun. Write the correct letter on the line.

1. deck _____   **a.** soldiers

2. pride _____   **b.** cookies

3. troop _____   **c.** cards

4. batch _____   **d.** lions

Name_____ Date_____

4.2 Plural Forms of Nouns That End with *x*, *s*, *z*, *ch*, *sh*, or *y*

The plural of a noun that ends in *x, s, z, ch,* or *sh* is formed by adding *-es* to the word. Some nouns end with a vowel and a *y*. The plural of these nouns is formed by adding *-s*. Some nouns end with a consonant and a *y*. The plural of these nouns is formed by changing the *y* to *i* and adding *-es*.

Singular Noun	Plural Noun	Spelling Rule
glass	glasses	(Add *-es*.)
key	keys	(Add *-s*.)
puppy	puppies	(Change *y* to *i* and add *-es*.)

Write the plural form of the noun in parentheses.

1. The people in my office have several (party) each year. _____

2. We like to celebrate different (holiday). _____

3. On Boss's Day, we bought gifts for our two (boss). _____

4. We gave them each two (box) of candy. _____

5. We ordered four (bunch) of flowers for the office. _____

6. We celebrate (birthday) at the end of each month. _____

7. Everyone has to make three (wish). _____

8. Everyone tells (story) about their favorite presents. _____

CRITICAL THINKING

Write a sentence using the plural form of one of the following nouns: *coach, day, story.*

_____

_____

Name_____ Date_____

4.2 Plural Forms of Nouns That End with *f*, *fe*, or *o*

Some nouns end with *f*, *ff,* or *fe*. The plural of some of these nouns is formed by adding -*s*. For others, change *f* to *v* and add -*s* or -*es*. Some nouns end with a vowel and an *o*. The plural of these nouns is formed by adding -*s*. Some nouns end with a consonant and an *o*. The plural of these nouns is formed by adding -*es*.

Singular Noun	Plural Noun	Spelling Rule
bluff	bluffs	(Add -*s*.)
wolf	wolves	(Change f to v and add -*es*.)
wife	wives	(Change f to v and add -*s*.)
zoo	zoos	(Add -*s*.)
hero	heroes	(Add -*es*.)

Write the plural form of the noun in parentheses.

1. My uncle likes to go to (rodeo). _____

2. My favorite animals are the (calf). _____

3. One cowboy always rolls up the (cuff) of his pants. _____

4. He also wears two (handkerchief) for good luck. _____

5. He puts his trophies on the (shelf) in his house. _____

CRITICAL THINKING

Use the plural form of the following words to write two sentences: *half, zoo.*

_____

_____

_____

_____

4.2 Plural Forms of Irregular Nouns

> Some plural nouns do not end with -s. These nouns become plural
> by changing other letters in the word. Some nouns are the same in
> the singular and plural forms.
>
> | Singular Noun | Plural Noun |
> | --- | --- |
> | woman | women |
> | ox | oxen |
> | sheep | sheep |

**Rewrite each sentence. Change the noun in parentheses to its
plural form.**

1. Many pioneer (man) farmed from morning to night.

_____

2. The (woman) washed the family's clothes by hand.

_____

3. The (child) helped their parents milk the cows and gather eggs.

_____

4. (Ox) were used to pull the plows and wagons.

_____

5. Some settlers raised (sheep).

_____

CRITICAL THINKING

**The plural nouns in the sentence below are spelled incorrectly.
Rewrite the sentence correctly.**

Two mouses just ran across my foots. _____

_____

4.3 Possessive Nouns

A **possessive noun** shows ownership or relationship. To form the possessive noun, add an **apostrophe** and an *-s* to most singular nouns. Add just an apostrophe to most plural nouns that end with *s*. Add an apostrophe and an *-s* to plural nouns that do not end with *s*.

Singular Noun	Plural Noun Ending in *-s*	Plural Noun Not Ending in *-s*
his friend's car	my sisters' room	the mice's hole

Rewrite each sentence. Change the noun in parentheses to its possessive form.

1. The (men) soccer team won the city finals.

_____

2. The (team) victory party was held on Sunday.

_____

3. We had the party at the (Pattersons) house.

_____

4. (Luis) girlfriend brought snacks.

_____

5. After the party, we went swimming in (Carl) pool.

_____

CRITICAL THINKING

**The possessive noun in the sentence below is incorrect.
Explain why.**

I saw two of my friend's pictures in the newspaper. _____

_____

▶ 4.4 Concrete and Abstract Nouns   Exercise 33

A **concrete noun** names something you can see, hear, touch, smell, or taste. Concrete nouns include people, places, and things. An **abstract noun** names an idea, quality, or feeling.

Concrete Noun	Abstract Noun
friend	loyalty
card	love

Circle the abstract noun in each row of words.

1. boat   lake   fun   fish

2. freedom   flag   bell   fireworks

3. beauty   rose   daisy   sunflower

4. song   love   book   pencil

5. truth   friend   judge   parent

6. money   wealth   car   diamonds

7. shot   doctor   nurse   sickness

8. shoes   clothes   fashion   hat

CRITICAL THINKING

Fill in the chart with concrete and abstract nouns of your own.

Concrete Noun	Abstract Noun

Name_____ Date_____

▶ 4.5 Writing: Using Noun Forms in Sentences

Exercise 34

Many sentences use different forms of nouns.

Follow the READ, PLAN, WRITE, and CHECK steps to write sentences using different noun forms. READ the tips below to help you understand the writing assignment.

READ   **Do you understand the assignment?**

- Read the assignment.
- Rewrite the assignment in your own words.
- Underline the key words.

Complete the writing assignments below.

1. What objects make you think of the United States? On a separate sheet of paper, write a sentence listing some objects that represent our country. Use concrete nouns.

_____

_____

_____

2. What do you think these objects mean? Write a sentence listing the qualities that these objects stand for. Use abstract nouns.

_____

_____

_____

PUTTING IT ALL TOGETHER

What are some of the symbols of the United States? On a separate sheet of paper, write a paragraph about both the objects that represent the United States and what these objects stand for. You may wish to use the sentences you have written above. Add other sentences to explain your ideas.

5.1 Identifying Personal Pronouns and Antecedents

Exercise 35

A **pronoun** is a word that takes the place of a noun. A **personal pronoun** identifies the speaker, the person spoken to, or the person or thing spoken about. An **antecedent** is a word or group of words that a pronoun refers to.

Personal Pronouns		
The speaker	The person spoken to	The person or thing spoken about
I, me, we, us	you	he, him, she, her, it, they, them

Ed, did you find the key? (*Ed* is the antecedent of *you*.)

Write the personal pronoun and antecedent in each sentence.

1. The students have a garden that they have planted. _____

2. The garden is large, and it has flowers and vegetables. _____

3. Maria is raising tulips because she enjoys flowers. _____

4. Helen asked Joe to help her pull some weeds. _____

5. Paul, do you think these tomatoes look ripe? _____

6. Maria said, "Paul, please give me a tomato." _____

CRITICAL THINKING

What would happen if you never used personal pronouns in your writing?

_____

_____

_____

_____

Name _____ Date _____

▶ 5.1 Pronoun-Antecedent Agreement   **Exercise 36**

> A pronoun must agree with its antecedent. The antecedent must be the same in number and person as the pronoun. In the examples below, the personal pronouns are underlined once. The antecedents are underlined twice.
>
> Carla lives far from school, so she takes the bus. (singular)
> Tim and Sue live nearby, so they always walk. (plural)
> Mr. García bikes to work whenever he has time. (masculine)
> Ms. Shay invited Ms. Lao to carpool with her. (feminine)

Write each sentence. Add a personal pronoun of your own. Remember that a pronoun must agree with its antecedent.

1. Russ lives in a city, but _____ is visiting a ranch.

2. Russ's cousin Anna taught _____ how to ride a horse.

3. Russ and Anna have fun when _____ ride horses together.

4. The horses are hungry after a ride, so Russ feeds _____.

5. Anna says _____ hopes to visit Russ in the city soon.

6. Anna can't wait to take _____ first train ride.

7. Russ said, "Anna, do _____ know how to get to the city?"

8. Anna said, "No. Please give _____ directions."

CRITICAL THINKING

The pronoun in the sentence below does not agree with its antecedent. Explain why it does not agree.

Dennis bought some shoes, and they also bought some socks.

_____

_____

_____

▶ 5.2 Reflexive Pronouns   Exercise 37

> A **reflexive pronoun** refers back to a noun or pronoun already
> named. A reflexive pronoun adds new information or gives extra
> importance to the word it refers to. A reflexive pronoun ends
> in *-self* or *-selves.*
>
>   Meg built the bookcase herself. (new information)
>
>   Meg herself built the bookcase. (extra importance)

Write the reflexive pronoun in each sentence.

1. Anika and Bob wanted to fix the bicycle themselves. _____

2. Anika herself thought of the idea. _____

3. Bob went to the library himself to get books about bicycles. _____

4. "You will have to buy the parts yourself," said Anika. _____

5. She said, "In the meantime, I will take off the flat tire myself." _____

6. They surprised themselves and fixed the bicycle easily. _____

CRITICAL THINKING

Add a reflexive pronoun of your own to the sentence below.

I _____ will help you with your project.

**Now explain whether the reflexive pronoun adds new
information or gives extra importance.**

_____

_____

_____

_____

5.3 Possessive Pronouns   Exercise 38

A **possessive pronoun** shows ownership or relationship. Some
possessive pronouns come before nouns. Other possessive
pronouns take the place of possessive nouns.

Possessive Pronouns That Come Before Nouns				Possessive Pronouns That Take the Place of Possessive Nouns			
my	your	his	her	mine	yours	his	hers
its	our	their		its	ours	theirs	

Write the correct possessive pronoun in each sentence.

1. Eric asked if (its, his) family could go hiking. _____

2. Eric's mom said they could go during (their, theirs) vacation. _____

3. (Your, Yours) idea is great! _____

4. We can take (our, ours) lunch and hike in the mountains. _____

5. I lost (mine, my) map of the mountain hiking trails. _____

6. The Greens have one, and we can borrow (their, theirs). _____

7. Can (my, mine) friend Alberto come with us? _____

8. Any friend of (your, yours) is welcome. _____

CRITICAL THINKING

**Rewrite the sentences. Replace the underlined words with
possessive pronouns.**

1. The small brown hiking boots are <u>Jayne's</u>. _____

_____

2. <u>Eric and Jayne's</u> dog must stay home. _____

_____

Name _____ Date _____

An **indefinite pronoun** takes the place of an unnamed noun.

Singular Indefinite Pronouns			Plural Indefinite Pronouns		
all	everybody	nothing	all	many	some
another	everyone	one	any	most	such
any	everything	other	both	none	
anybody	most	some	few	several	
anyone	neither	somebody			
anything	nobody	someone			
each	none	something			
either	no one	such			

Write the indefinite pronouns in each sentence. Some sentences have more than one.

1. Both of these bus lines will take you downtown. _____

2. One is an express, and the other makes local stops. _____

3. The express is used by most of the neighbors. _____

4. Because few take the local, you should get a seat. _____

5. Nobody likes to drive downtown. _____

6. After all, does anybody enjoy traffic jams? _____

7. Someone told me about a street fair downtown. _____

8. There will be something for everyone. _____

CRITICAL THINKING

Choose two of the following pronouns: *anything, nothing, many, some*. Write two sentences using the words you chose.

_____

_____

_____

5.5 Writing: Using Pronouns and Antecedents in Sentences

Exercise 40

Pronouns help writers avoid repeating the same words.

Follow the READ, PLAN, WRITE, and CHECK steps to write sentences using pronouns. READ the tips below to help you understand the writing assignment.

READ **Do you understand the assignment?**

- Read the assignment.
- Rewrite the assignment in your own words.
- Underline the key words.

Complete the writing assignments below.

1. Who is one person you would turn to for advice? Write a sentence describing two things about this person. Use at least one personal pronoun.

_____

_____

_____

2. Why would you ask this person for advice? Write a sentence telling why you trust this person. Give two reasons. Use at least one reflexive pronoun.

_____

_____

_____

PUTTING IT ALL TOGETHER

What kind of person might give good advice? On a separate sheet of paper, write a paragraph about someone you might ask for advice. You may wish to use the sentences you wrote above. Add other sentences to explain your ideas.

▶ 6.1 Interrogative Pronouns

An **interrogative pronoun** asks a question. Look at the chart below
to see how each interrogative pronoun is used.

Interrogative Pronoun	How It Is Used
who, whom	refers to a person or people (Use *who* when referring to a subject. Use *whom* when referring to someone else.)
whose	refers to ownership or relationship
what	refers to people, places, things, events, and ideas
which	refers to a choice between two or more people, places, things, events, and ideas

Write the correct interrogative pronoun in each sentence.

1. (Whom, Who) heard the weather report? _____

2. Tell me (what, which) the weather reporter said. _____

3. I do not know (which, what) we should do if it rains. _____

4. To (whom, who) did you send invitations? _____

5. (Which, What) will the weather be on Sunday? _____

6. (Who, Whom) thinks we should go on Saturday? _____

7. (Which, What) one of you can call everyone? _____

8. Here is a list of food to bring. (Whose, Whom) is it? _____

CRITICAL THINKING

**The interrogative pronoun is used incorrectly in the sentence
below. Explain why it is incorrect.**

What of the two parks is closer to home?

_____

_____

Name_____ Date_____

A **demonstrative pronoun** points out one or more nouns. Look at the chart below to see how each demonstrative pronoun is used.

Demonstrative Pronoun	How It Is Used
this	refers to a noun that is singular and nearby
that	refers to a noun that is singular and farther away
these	refers to a noun that is plural and nearby
those	refers to a noun that is plural and farther away

Add a demonstrative pronoun of your own to each sentence.

1. _____ is my house we are standing in front of.

2. _____ are the flowers I planted right here.

3. _____ is my aunt's house across the street.

4. _____ are my cousins sitting on their porch.

5. Are _____ your brothers next door?

6. _____ is my sister sitting with them.

CRITICAL THINKING

Write two sentences of your own. Use a different demonstrative pronoun in each sentence.

_____

_____

_____

_____

_____

6.3 Relative Pronouns   **Exercise 43**

A **relative pronoun** connects a noun or pronoun with a group of words that tells more about it. Look at the chart below to see how each relative pronoun is used.

Relative Pronoun	How It Is Used
who, whom	refers to a person or people (Use who when referring to a subject. Use whom when referring to someone else.)
whose	refers to ownership or relationship
that, which	refers to places and things (Use that when adding necessary information. Use which when adding information that is not necessary to the meaning of the sentence.)

Add the correct relative pronoun to each sentence.

1. The woman _____ you met is running for mayor.

2. She is the one _____ picture was on the front page.

3. She has a plan _____ will improve the bus system.

4. The man, _____ is on the stage, is also running for mayor.

5. He, too, may have ideas _____ would be good for the city.

6. I'll listen to his speech, _____ begins in five minutes.

7. Everyone should vote in the election, _____ is in October.

8. For _____ will you vote?

CRITICAL THINKING

Replace the underlined word with a relative pronoun.
Then combine the two sentences.

Our best player is Patti. <u>Patti</u> scored 20 points in last night's game.

▶ 6.4 Writing: Using Pronouns That Ask and Point in Sentences

Exercise 44

Pronouns help you ask questions, point out things, or connect groups of words.

Follow the READ, PLAN, WRITE, and CHECK steps to help you write sentences with interrogative, demonstrative, and relative pronouns. The tips below will help you PLAN your writing.

PLAN   **Gather your ideas and organize them.**

- The questions in the assignments will help you gather your ideas.

- Use a sunburst diagram to organize your ideas.

Complete the writing assignments below.

1. Someone who lived over 100 years ago was transported to your city. Write a sentence explaining some things you would show this person. What would be interesting for this person to see? Use at least one relative pronoun.

_____

_____

_____

2. Write a sentence explaining what you would ask the visitor about the past. What things about the past would you want to know? Use an interrogative pronoun.

_____

_____

_____

PUTTING IT ALL TOGETHER

What changes have taken place in the last 100 years? On a separate sheet of paper, write a paragraph about the changes someone from the past might see today. You may wish to use the sentences you wrote above. Add other sentences to explain your ideas.

▶ 7.1 What Is a Verb?

A **verb** is a word that shows action or a state of being. Sometimes, a verb expresses an action that cannot be seen or heard. Every sentence must have a verb. A sentence may have more than one verb.

Sometimes Ryan <u>cooks</u> breakfast. (shows action)
He <u>is</u> an excellent cook. (shows state of being)
Ryan <u>likes</u> to cook. (action that cannot be seen or heard)
He also <u>washes</u> and <u>dries</u> the dishes. (more than one verb)

Write the verb in each sentence below.

1. Miguel and his father went to the fishing pond. _____

2. Miguel put bait on his hook. _____

3. Then he threw the line into the water. _____

4. He waited for a long time. _____

5. Finally, he felt a tug on his line. _____

6. It was a huge fish! _____

7. Miguel dreamed of a delicious fish dinner. _____

8. Then the line broke. _____

CRITICAL THINKING

Read each sentence below. Explain the difference between the two kinds of verbs.

Harry parks the car.   Lilly is a race car driver.

_____

_____

_____

_____

▶ 7.2 Action Verbs   Exercise 46

> An **action verb** expresses physical or mental action. In the examples below, the action verb is underlined.
>
> Jen <u>walked</u> to school. (physical action)
> She <u>thought</u> about her test in history. (mental action)

Write the action verb in each sentence.

1. I went to the mall with my friends last weekend. _____

2. We laughed all day. _____

3. We saw some of our other friends there. _____

4. Many people go to the mall on Saturday. _____

5. We shopped at some of the stores. _____

6. Emily bought a new pair of shoes. _____

7. Rebecca wanted a new swimsuit. _____

8. Darryl found a tape of his favorite band. _____

9. We ate lunch at the food court. _____

10. Then we watched a movie at the theater. _____

11. The movie lasted over two hours. _____

12. Everyone really enjoyed the movie. _____

CRITICAL THINKING

Read the words below. Circle the verbs that show mental action.

admire	stop	love	decide	sit
eat	believe	freeze	think	wait

Name _____ Date _____

▶ 7.3 Linking Verbs   Exercise 47

> A **linking verb** expresses what is or what seems to be. It links the
> subject of a sentence with a word that describes the subject.
>
> | Common Linking Verbs | | | | | |
> | --- | --- | --- | --- | --- | --- |
> | be | are | act | feel | remain | sound |
> | am | was | appear | grow | seem | stay |
> | is | were | become | look | smell | taste |

Write the linking verb in each sentence.

1. Many works of art are in this museum. _____

2. Some of the paintings look very beautiful. _____

3. Others seem strange. _____

4. This one appears very old. _____

5. The museum is very big. _____

6. We grew tired after awhile. _____

7. We were hungry so we ate lunch. _____

8. Italian food sounded good to everyone. _____

9. The food in the restaurant smelled great! _____

10. The pizza tasted terrific! _____

CRITICAL THINKING
Write a sentence using each verb as a linking verb.

1. (act) _____

2. (remain) _____

3. (seem) _____

Name_____ Date_____

> The **tense** of a verb tells when the action of the verb occurs. A verb
> can express action in the past, present, or future tense. A verb in the
> **present tense** describes action that is happening now or that is repeated.
>
>   I <u>see</u> the sign across the street. (action happening now)
>   This store <u>opens</u> at 10:00. (repeated action)

Write the present tense verb in each sentence.

1. Spaghetti is my favorite meal. _____

2. My mom cooks the best spaghetti. _____

3. It smells wonderful. _____

4. Andy likes sausage with his spaghetti. _____

5. My spaghetti has meatballs on top. _____

6. The spaghetti curls around the meatballs. _____

7. Steam rises from my plate. _____

8. My hungry stomach rumbles. _____

9. We smile at the sight of the food. _____

10. Everyone enjoys spaghetti night. _____

CRITICAL THINKING

**Write two sentences about your favorite food. Use present tense
verbs in your sentences.**

_____

_____

_____

_____

▶ 7.5 Making Subjects and Verbs Agree   Exercise 49

In the present tense, most verbs have a singular and a plural form. The singular form ends in -*s*. The plural form does not end in -*s*.

The subject and the verb of a sentence must agree. When a singular subject is used in a sentence, a singular verb must be used. When the sentence has a plural subject, a plural verb must be used.

Jimmy works at the movie theater. (singular)
My other friends work at the grocery store. (plural)

Write each sentence. Use the correct form of the verb in parentheses.

1. Many people (visit, visits) this beach each summer.

_____

2. The sun (shine, shines) brightly over the water.

_____

3. The waves (crash, crashes) along the shore.

_____

4. The water (feel, feels) very warm.

_____

5. The lifeguard (watch, watches) all of the swimmers.

_____

CRITICAL THINKING

Decide if the subject and verb in the sentence below agree.
Explain why the sentence is correct or incorrect.

My friends tells the funniest jokes.

_____

_____

▶ 7.5 Subject-Verb Agreement with Indefinite Pronouns and Compound Subjects

Indefinite pronouns can be the subject of a sentence. The verb must agree with the indefinite pronoun. If the pronoun refers to one person or thing, it is singular. If it refers to more than one person or thing, it is plural.

<u>Someone</u> <u>knows</u> the answer. (singular)
<u>Many</u> <u>know</u> the answer. (plural)

Some sentences have two or more subjects. If the subjects are joined by *and*, use a plural verb. If *or* or *nor* joins the subjects, use a verb that agrees with the noun or pronoun closest to the verb.

My best <u>friend</u> and <u>I</u> <u>like</u> English class. (plural)
The students or the <u>teacher</u> <u>reads</u> the poem. (singular)

Write the correct form of the verb in parentheses.

1. The board members and the mayor (plan) the event. _____

2. Each (hope) for a big crowd. _____

3. Many (look) forward to the event all year. _____

4. Either fireworks or a band (end) the show. _____

5. Everyone (stay) until the end. _____

6. Either the fire chief or the police chief (give) a speech. _____

CRITICAL THINKING

Read the following sentence. Tell why it is incorrect.

Everybody enjoy the rides at the fair.

_____

_____

_____

Name_____   Date_____

 7.5 Subject-Verb Agreement with   **Exercise 51**
     Titles and Amounts

> If the title of a book or movie is the subject of a sentence, use a
> singular verb form. If the name of a country or organization is the
> subject of a sentence, use a singular verb. When an amount is the
> subject of a sentence, use a singular verb if the amount is a single
> unit. Use a plural verb if the amount is individual units.
>
>   _Oliver_ <u>is</u> a movie about a young orphan boy. (singular)
>   The <u>Drama Club</u> <u>meets</u> on Thursday. (singular)
>   <u>Two thirds</u> of the apple pie <u>is</u> gone. (singular)
>   <u>Three</u> of the students <u>study</u> for the test. (plural)

**Write each sentence. Use the correct form of the verb
in parentheses.**

1. _Think to Win_ (teach) people how to play chess.

_____

2. York College (have) a chess play-off each year.

_____

3. Three quarters of the players (be) teenagers.

_____

4. Twelve of the judges (watch) the players.

_____

5. One half of the play-off game (be) on television.

_____

CRITICAL THINKING

Write a sentence of your own. Use the name of your school as
the subject of the sentence. Use a present tense verb.

_____

7.6 Past Tense Verb Forms

A **past tense** verb describes an action or state of being that has already happened. Many past tense verbs are made by adding *-d* or *-ed* to the present tense plural form.

Present Tense Verb	Past Tense Verb
Today, I *play* soccer.	Yesterday, I *played* soccer.
Today, I *practice* hard.	Yesterday, I *practiced* hard.

Write the past tense verb form in each sentence.

1. Each student typed a report. _____

2. Everyone printed his or her report. _____

3. Then we each picked a partner. _____

4. The partners exchanged papers. _____

5. We looked for mistakes in the other person's paper. _____

6. We marked the mistakes in red ink. _____

7. We talked about our mistakes. _____

8. Each student corrected his or her report. _____

9. The teacher asked for our papers. _____

10. The teacher graded the reports. _____

CRITICAL THINKING

Read the sentences below. Explain how changing the verb tense changes the meaning of the sentence.

Gary calls every night.   Gary called every night.

_____

_____

Name _____ Date _____

▶ 7.7 Irregular Past Tense Verb Forms   **Exercise 53**

Verbs that do not form the past tense by adding *-d* or *-ed* are called **irregular verbs**. In the boxes below are some present tense verb forms followed by their irregular past tense forms.

Present	Past
come	came
drink	drank
give	gave
go	went
run	ran

Present	Past
sleep	slept
speak	spoke
steal	stole
take	took
ride	rode

Write the past tense form of the verb in parentheses.

1. A group of friends (take) a trip to the park. _____

2. They (ride) their bicycles to the park. _____

3. Nina (go) to see the new fountain. _____

4. Timothy (sleep) under a tree. _____

5. The officer (give) the bike riders a warning. _____

6. She (speak) to them about bicycle safety. _____

CRITICAL THINKING
Write the past tense verb form of the words in the chart.

Present Tense	Irregular Past Tense
bring	
sing	
write	

7.8 Writing: Using Verbs in Sentences   Exercise 54

Every complete sentence contains at least one verb. Verbs can show action or a state of being in the present tense or in the past tense.

Follow the READ, PLAN, WRITE, and CHECK steps to use verbs correctly in sentences. The tips below will help you PLAN your writing.

PLAN   **Gather your ideas and organize them.**

- Read the assignments and discuss your ideas with a partner.
- Use a chart to organize your ideas.

Complete the writing assignments below.

1. Write two sentences about what a person can do to be a good friend. Explain why these actions are important. Use at least one linking verb and one action verb in your sentences.

_____

_____

_____

2. Write two sentences about something that you have done to be a good friend. Tell what you did and explain why. Use at least one linking verb and one action verb in your sentences.

_____

_____

_____

PUTTING IT ALL TOGETHER

What can you do to show your friendship to others? On a separate sheet of paper, write a paragraph about how to be a good friend. You may want to use the sentences you have written above. Add other sentences to explain your ideas.

Name _____ Date _____

▶ 8.1 Identifying Verb Phrases   Exercise 55

In a **verb phrase**, there is one **main verb** and at least one
helping verb. The main verb tells what happens or what is.
The helping verb helps the main verb.

The forms of the verb *to be* often serve as helping verbs. The forms
of the verb *to be* are in the box below.

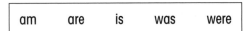

| am | are | is | was | were |

In the example below, the main verb is underlined once. The
helping verb is underlined twice.

Jimmy <u>was</u> <u>speaking</u> to the group.

**Write the verb phrase in each sentence. Draw one line under
each main verb. Draw two lines under each helping verb.**

1. Everyone is working on the old house. _____

2. I am cleaning the floors. _____

3. Doug and Karen are painting the walls. _____

4. Zach is repairing a broken door. _____

5. Several people are washing the windows. _____

6. Jack was mowing the grass. _____

7. Cindy and Wesley were pulling weeds. _____

8. Alyssa is building a new mailbox. _____

CRITICAL THINKING

**Write two sentences about things that are happening now.
Use a main verb and a form of *to be* as a helping verb.**

_____

_____

8.1 Using Present Participles   Exercise 56

> A **present participle** is a verb form that shows continuing action.
> It is formed by adding *-ing* to the plural form of the verb.
>
> Present participles always use a form of the helping verb *to be*. If
> the helping verb is *am*, *is*, or *are*, the verb phrase shows continuing
> action in the present. If the helping verb is *was* or *were*, the verb
> phrase shows continuing action in the past.
>
>   Everyone <u>is reading</u>. (shows continuing action in the present)
>   The students <u>were listening</u>. (shows continuing action in the past)

**Change the verb to a verb phrase in the sentences below. Use a
form of the verb *to be* and the present participle.**

1. I write a long letter. _____

2. My pen runs out of ink. _____

3. The pencils get dull. _____

4. My friends expect a letter. _____

5. I look for their addresses. _____

6. My sister gives me stamps. _____

7. I mail the letter. _____

8. I wait for a response. _____

CRITICAL THINKING

Explain the difference between the two sentences below.

I am hurrying to class.   I was hurrying to class.

_____

_____

_____

Name _____ Date _____

▶ 8.2 Verb Phrases with *To Have*   Exercise 57

A **past participle** shows completed action. It is usually formed by
adding *-d, -ed, -n,* or *-en* to the plural form of the verb. Some past
participles are formed from irregular verbs. The helping verbs *have,
has,* and *had* are used with past participles.

Plural Verb Form	Past Participle
know	(have) known
break	(has) broken
close	(had) closed

**Rewrite each sentence. Change the verb to a verb phrase.
Use a form of the verb *to have* and the past participle.**

1. My favorite author wrote another book.

_____

2. Many people read his first three books.

_____

3. He sold over a million copies in all.

_____

4. I met him in person at a book signing.

_____

5. He wrote his first book when he was 16 years old.

_____

CRITICAL THINKING

Explain when to use the different verb forms of *to have*.

_____

_____

▶ 8.3 Verb Phrases with *To Do*   Exercise 58

> Some verb phrases use a form of *to do* as a helping verb. The helping verb *to do* is used in questions, with the word *not*, and to add emphasis to a sentence. The verb phrases are underlined in the sentences below.
>
> <u>Did</u> you <u>find</u> my book? (in a question)
> I <u>did</u> not <u>find</u> your book. (with the word *not*)
> I <u>did find</u> your keys, though. (for emphasis)

Write the verb phrase in each sentence.

1. I do like sunny days. _____

2. The sun does feel warm today. _____

3. Did you remember the sunscreen? _____

4. I do sunburn easily. _____

5. This park does not have a beautiful view of the river. _____

6. We did enjoy our picnic in the park. _____

CRITICAL THINKING

Use a form of *to do* as a helping verb to write three sentences. Write the first sentence as a question. Use the word *not* in the second sentence. Use the helping verb *to do* to add emphasis in the third sentence.

1. Question: _____

_____

2. With *not*: _____

_____

3. Emphasis: _____

_____

Name _____ Date _____

 8.4 Other Helping Verbs   **Exercise 59**

> Some helping verbs are used to change the meaning of a sentence.
> The helping verbs *can, could, may, might, must, should,* and *would*
> are all followed by a plural verb form. In the examples below, the
> verb phrases are underlined.
>
>   They <u>must dance</u> well to win the contest.
>   <u>Should</u> we <u>wait</u> for the scores?

Write the verb phrase in each sentence.

1. The movie should start any minute. _____

2. We must hurry. _____

3. We might miss the beginning. _____

4. Can you believe the size of this theater? _____

5. Either Ken or I could sit next to you. _____

6. I may want popcorn during the movie. _____

7. Can we share the popcorn? _____

8. Andy might want butter on his. _____

9. This movie could be very good. _____

10. Must they show so many previews? _____

CRITICAL THINKING

**Read the two sentences below. The helping verb has been
changed in the second sentence. Explain how the helping verb
changes the meaning of the sentence.**

You could find a job.   You must find a job.

_____

_____

8.5 Verb Phrases and *Not*

> The word *not* is a part of speech called an adverb. It usually comes between a helping verb and a main verb in a sentence. It is not part of the verb phrase. The verb phrases have been underlined in the examples below.
>
> I <u>did</u> not <u>read</u> that book.
> Barb <u>has</u> not <u>read</u> that book.

Write the verb phrase in each sentence.

1. In the story, the hero did not act afraid. _____

2. He did not care about the danger. _____

3. The trapped man could not move. _____

4. The hero was not thinking about himself. _____

5. He could not leave the man there. _____

6. Later, the hero would not accept a reward. _____

7. He did not want any attention. _____

8. The man did not know his name. _____

9. I have not read the end of the story. _____

10. I may not finish the story today. _____

CRITICAL THINKING

Think about something you should have done yesterday but did not do. Write a sentence about what you did not do. Use a verb phrase and *not*.

_____

_____

_____

Name _____ Date _____

 8.6 Future Tense   **Exercise 61**

> A verb in the **future tense** shows action or being that will happen in the future. To form the future tense, use the helping verbs *will* or *shall* with a plural verb form. The word *not* or the subject of a question may come in the middle of a future tense verb phrase. In the examples below, the future tense verb phrases are underlined.
>
>   I <u>will be</u> home this afternoon.
>   We <u>shall meet</u> you later.
>   <u>Will</u> you <u>meet</u> me tomorrow?
>   I <u>will</u> not <u>meet</u> you tomorrow.

Write the verb phrase in each sentence.

1. The meeting will be about a new town project. _____

2. The town leaders will ask for everyone's help. _____

3. Many people will attend the meeting. _____

4. Soon, we shall have a new town square. _____

5. The meeting will not start on time. _____

6. Will you take notes for me? _____

CRITICAL THINKING

Choose one of the following verbs: *listen, drive, shop.* Use the verb
to write a sentence in the present tense, past tense, and future tense.

1. Present Tense: _____

_____

2. Past Tense: _____

_____

3. Future Tense: _____

_____

Name _____ Date _____

A sentence is in the **active voice** if the subject of a sentence performs the action of the verb. A sentence is in the **passive voice** if the action of the verb is done *to* the subject. The passive voice always has a verb phrase with a form of the verb *to be* and a past participle.

Hal <u>wrote</u> the speech. (active voice)
The speech <u>was written</u> by Hal. (passive voice)

Rewrite each sentence. Change the verb phrase from the passive voice to the active voice.

1. Troy was given a ride to the race by Mrs. Moore.

_____

2. The final race was won by Jason.

_____

3. Our team was given the most points by the judges.

_____

4. The winning team was cheered by the crowd.

_____

5. A medal was given to each team member by the judge.

_____

CRITICAL THINKING

Why should writers use the active voice in their writing as much as possible?

_____

_____

_____

Name _____ Date _____

 8.8 Writing: Using Verb Phrases in Sentences   **Exercise 63**

Many sentences use verb phrases. They help express when an action takes place.

Follow the READ, PLAN, WRITE, and CHECK steps to write sentences with verb phrases. The questions below will help you CHECK your writing.

CHECK   How can you improve your writing?

- Do your sentences answer the assignment?
- Did you use helping verbs correctly?
- How can you make your writing clearer?

Complete the writing assignments below.

1. Write two sentences about a useful invention. What do you think is a good invention? Why do you think this invention is useful? Use helping verbs in your sentences.

_____

_____

_____

2. Write two sentences about an invention that you do not think is useful. Explain why you think it is not a good invention. Use helping verbs in your sentences.

_____

_____

_____

PUTTING IT ALL TOGETHER

How do inventions help people? On a separate sheet of paper, write a paragraph about two inventions. Tell about an invention that is useful and one that is not useful. You may wish to use the sentences you have written above. Add other sentences to explain your ideas.

9.1 Simple Subjects and Simple Predicates   Exercise 64

> The **simple subject** is the part of the subject that is a noun
> or pronoun. The **simple predicate** is the part of the predicate
> that is a verb or verb phrase. In the examples below, each
> simple subject is underlined once. Each simple predicate is
> underlined twice.
>
>   A <u>friend</u> of mine <u>found</u> ten dollars on the ground.
>   The <u>money</u> <u>must have fallen</u> from someone's pocket.

Write the simple subject and simple predicate of each sentence.

1. The day was perfect for a sailboat ride. _____

2. A strong wind blew the boat across the lake. _____

3. The waves gently rocked the boat. _____

4. The sun shone brightly on the water. _____

5. Many tiny fish were swimming near the boat. _____

6. A few seagulls were flying overhead. _____

7. Only a few boats were on the water. _____

8. Everything seemed calm and peaceful. _____

CRITICAL THINKING

Choose a simple subject and a simple predicate from the boxes.
Write a sentence of your own using the words you chose.

Simple Subjects
balloon   bubble

Simple Predicates
popped   is floating

_____

_____

_____

9.2 Identifying Direct Objects   **Exercise 65**

A **direct object** is a noun or a pronoun that receives the action of a verb. A direct object comes after the verb or verb phrase. It always follows an action verb. In the examples below, the direct objects are underlined.

Sean chose a <u>table</u> near the window.

Julian ate <u>that</u>.

Write the direct object in each sentence.

1. We rented skates at the skating rink. _____

2. We saw Christi there. _____

3. We really surprised her. _____

4. I asked Juanita if she wanted a snack. _____

5. I bought a drink for both of us. _____

6. Juanita ate some popcorn. _____

7. Felix enjoyed the music. _____

8. They played many great songs. _____

9. Felix wore his blue skates. _____

10. Felix and I made some new friends. _____

CRITICAL THINKING

Circle each sentence that has a direct object. Explain how you can tell if a sentence has a direct object.

Mark hit the ball.   The ball flew over the fence.

Mark scored a home run.   The fans cheered loudly.

_____

_____

▶ 9.3 Indirect Objects

> An **indirect object** tells *to whom* or *for whom* an action is done. It is a noun or a pronoun. An indirect object comes after the verb and before the direct object in a sentence. It always follows an action verb. An indirect object never comes after the word *for* or *to*. In the examples below, the indirect objects are underlined.
>
>   Michelle gave <u>me</u> a present.
>   I showed <u>everyone</u> the gift.

Draw one line under each indirect object.

1. Cassandra sent my family an invitation to dinner.

2. Cassandra's mother cooked us a wonderful dinner.

3. Mrs. Jackson served everyone a large helping.

4. I brought Mrs. Jackson a pie for dessert.

5. Amy made them a salad.

6. After dinner, Cassandra showed Amy her car.

7. Cassandra's parents bought her a car for her birthday.

8. Cassandra gave me a ride to school the next day.

CRITICAL THINKING

Rewrite each sentence. Change the sentence to include an indirect object. Draw one line under the indirect object.

1. Cheryl bought some stamps for me. _____

_____

2. I handed the package to the mail carrier. _____

_____

Name _____ Date _____

▶ 9.4 Object Complements   **Exercise 67**

> An **object complement** renames or tells more about the direct
> object. An object complement follows a direct object and refers to
> it. An object complement is a noun or an adjective. In the
> examples below, the object complements are underlined.
>
> They made him <u>leader</u> of the group.
>
> He proved himself <u>trustworthy</u>.

Draw one line under each object complement.

1. We found the game interesting to watch.

2. The close score made the game exciting.

3. The players called that play-off game exhausting.

4. They made Bobby captain of the team.

5. The coach has always considered him a leader.

6. The school elected Mr. Hernández *Coach of the Year*.

7. Everyone found the award dinner memorable.

8. The team considered the trophy special for our school.

9. The coaches named Ricky *Most Improved Player* for the season.

10. I will title my essay *Our Championship Year*.

CRITICAL THINKING

Add an object complement of your own to the sentences below.

1. The letter made me _____.

2. I found the movie _____.

3. She called the dog _____.

▶ 9.5 Predicate Nominatives   Exercise 68

> A **predicate nominative** renames, describes, or identifies the
> subject of a sentence. The predicate nominative is a noun or a
> pronoun. It follows a linking verb or verb phrase. In the example
> below, the linking verb is underlined once. The predicate
> nominative is underlined twice.
>
>   History is my best subject.

**Draw one line under each linking verb. Draw two lines under
each predicate nominative.**

1. That girl is a new student.

2. Her name is Latisha.

3. She is my lab partner in science class.

4. Jackie is her older sister.

5. Jackie and Latisha are my neighbors.

6. They were students at Riverside High.

7. Mr. Atkins was Latisha's science teacher at her old school.

8. Latisha and I became friends quickly.

CRITICAL THINKING

**Decide whether each sentence has a predicate nominative or
a direct object. Circle only the sentences with a predicate
nominative.**

This watch was a gift.   My mother gave it to me.

She bought the watch last week.   It is a sports watch.

**Explain how you can tell the difference between a predicate
nominative and a direct object.**

_____

_____

Name _____ Date _____

> Many sentences contain a direct object and an indirect object. Others have an object complement or a predicate nominative.
>
> Follow the READ, PLAN, WRITE, and CHECK steps to write sentences using these sentence patterns. The tips below will help you PLAN your writing.
>
> PLAN   **Gather your ideas and organize them.**
>
> - The questions in the assignments will help you gather your ideas.
> - Use a chart to organize your ideas.

Complete the writing assignments below.

1. Write two sentences that describe a time when you ate something that you did not like. What food did you try, and why did you try it? Use a direct object and an indirect object.

_____

_____

_____

2. Write two sentences that describe how you reacted to the food, and why. How did the food make you feel? Use at least one predicate nominative and one object complement.

_____

_____

_____

PUTTING IT ALL TOGETHER

Why can it be good and bad to try new foods? On a separate sheet of paper, write a paragraph about trying new foods. You may wish to use the sentences you have written above. Add other sentences to complete the paragraph.

Name _____ Date _____

An **adjective** describes a noun or pronoun. It usually tells *what kind*, *which one*, or *how many*. An adjective often comes before the word it describes.

    Karen writes <u>mystery</u> stories. (tells *what kind*)
    <u>That</u> story was written last year. (tells *which one*)
    She has written <u>eleven</u> stories in all. (tells *how many*)

Write the adjectives in the sentences. Some sentences have more than one.

1. My favorite season is fall. _____

2. I see many red and yellow leaves. _____

3. Farmers have good crops this fall. _____

4. Some ripe vegetables have been harvested. _____

5. I bought two huge pumpkins. _____

6. I plan to make three pumpkin pies. _____

7. I enjoy crisp breezes and cool nights. _____

8. People wear beautiful sweaters and light jackets. _____

9. Winter days will be here in several months. _____

10. I love cold weather, warm fires, and hot cider. _____

CRITICAL THINKING

Read the sentences below. Circle the sentence in which *library* **is used as an adjective. Explain how you know it is used as an adjective.**

I am going to the library.   I just received my library card.

_____

_____

Name _____ Date _____

 10.2 Articles **Exercise 71**

> An **article** always comes before the noun it describes. *The* is a definite article. It refers to a specific noun or nouns. *A* and *an* are indefinite articles. They refer to any one of a group of things. *An* is used before a word that begins with a vowel sound.
>
> <u>The</u> day passed quickly. (definite article)
> <u>A</u> day has 24 hours. (indefinite article)
> <u>An</u> hour is enough. (indefinite article before vowel sound)

Circle the correct article in parentheses for each sentence.

1. Darlene is (a, an) honest person.

2. She found (a, an) wallet on (the, an) ground.

3. She asked (the, a) people around her if it was theirs.

4. No one said that they had lost (a, an) wallet.

5. She saw (a, an) airline ticket and (a, an) driver's license inside.

6. Darlene looked in (a, an) phone book and called (the, a) owner.

7. (An, The) man was very grateful.

8. He thanked Darlene and offered her (a, an) small reward.

9. Darlene did not accept (the, an) reward.

10. Doing (a, an) good deed was enough thanks for her.

CRITICAL THINKING

Circle the correct articles in parentheses for the sentence below. Then explain why you chose those articles.

Albert saw (a, an) airplane flying across (the, a) sky.

_____

_____

► 10.3 Predicate Adjectives   **Exercise 72**

> A **predicate adjective** describes the noun or pronoun that is the subject of the sentence. It comes after a form of the verb *to be* or another linking verb. The predicate adjective is underlined in the example below.
>
>   That movie seemed very <u>long</u>.

Write the predicate adjective in each sentence. Then write the noun it describes. There may be more than one predicate adjective in a sentence.

1. Everything looks wonderful. _____

2. The room is quiet and dark. _____

3. The food smells delicious. _____

4. I am so hungry. _____

5. Raymond will be a little late. _____

6. His day was very busy at work. _____

7. Dinner is finally ready. _____

8. The table is full of food. _____

9. It looks terrific! _____

10. The soup tastes hot and creamy. _____

CRITICAL THINKING

Choose a friend to describe. Write two positive sentences about your friend. Use linking verbs and predicate adjectives.

_____

_____

_____

Name _____ Date _____

> A **proper adjective** refers to a particular person, place, thing, event, or idea. It is formed from a proper noun. A proper adjective begins with a capital letter. In the example below, the proper adjective is underlined once. The noun it describes is underlined twice.
>
> San Francisco is famous for its <u>Victorian</u> <u>houses</u>.

Draw one line under the proper adjective in each sentence.
Draw two lines under the noun it describes.

1. The film showed many interesting European sights.

2. The Spanish city of Madrid is one of the places it showed.

3. We saw pictures of tulips and Dutch windmills.

4. Some English castles are hundreds of years old.

5. The Greek islands look beautiful.

6. The pictures of the Swiss mountains were amazing.

7. The French countryside seems so peaceful.

8. The film showed several Austrian villages.

9. Moscow, the Russian capital, is a very large city.

10. The autobahn, a famous German highway, has no speed limit.

CRITICAL THINKING

Rewrite each sentence below to include a proper adjective.

1. My grandfather gave me some money from Japan.

_____

2. My teacher knows a lot about the history of America.

_____

▶ 10.5 Adding *-er* and *-est* to Adjectives   Exercise 74

An adjective can be used to compare two or more nouns. An adjective that compares two items is called a **comparative adjective**. It usually ends in *-er*. An adjective that compares three or more items is called a **superlative adjective**. It usually ends in *-est*.

Jonathan is <u>older</u> than Craig. (comparative)

Jonathan is the <u>oldest</u> player on his team. (superlative)

Write the correct form of the adjective for each sentence.

1. We moved to a (bigger, biggest) apartment. _____

2. Of the three bedrooms, mine is the (smaller, smallest). _____

3. My brother's room is (larger, largest) than mine. _____

4. My room is the (brighter, brightest) of all. _____

5. I will keep my room the (cleaner, cleanest) of all. _____

6. The (nicer, nicest) room of all is the living room. _____

7. This carpet is (newer, newest) than our old carpet. _____

8. We live (farther, farthest) from school than we did before. _____

9. It will take me (longer, longest) to get to school now. _____

10. Now, we are (closer, closest) to my mom's office. _____

CRITICAL THINKING

Deirdre is 14 years old, Mike is 16, and Shawn is 18. Write a sentence that compares their ages using comparative and superlative adjectives.

_____

_____

_____

10.5 Using *More, Most, Less,* and *Least*   Exercise 75

> *More, most, less,* and *least* are used with adjectives that have several syllables. Look at the chart below to see how each adjective is used.
>
> | Adjectives | How They Are Used |
> |---|---|
> | *more* and *less* | to compare two items |
> | *most* and *least* | to compare three or more items |

Rewrite each sentence. Use *more, most, less,* or *least* with the adjective in parentheses.

1. This book is (interesting) than that one.

_____

2. I think this one is (difficult) to understand than that one.

_____

3. This author is the (talented) writer I have ever read.

_____

4. This book has sold many copies and is his (successful) work.

_____

5. I think that book is the (exciting) thing I have ever read.

_____

CRITICAL THINKING

The sentence below uses a superlative adjective incorrectly. Explain why it is incorrect. Rewrite it correctly.

Between these two shirts, this one is the most expensive.

_____

_____

Name_____ Date_____

10.5 Using Other Comparative Adjectives Exercise 76

> The adjectives *good* and *bad* change form when they are used to compare things. The forms of the adjective *good* are *good, better,* and *best.* The forms of the adjective *bad* are *bad, worse,* and *worst.* Use *better* and *worse* when comparing two things. Use *best* and *worst* when comparing three or more things.
>
> This store has <u>better prices</u> than that store. (comparative)
> This road has <u>worse traffic</u> than that one. (comparative)
> This store has the <u>best prices</u> of all. (superlative)
> This road has the <u>worst traffic</u> in the city. (superlative)

Rewrite each sentence. Use the correct form of the adjective in parentheses.

1. The weather last winter was (good) than the weather this winter.

_____

2. Do you think this storm will be (bad) than the one last week?

_____

3. This station has the (good) weather reports of all the stations.

_____

4. I think the storm is going to be (bad) tonight than it is now.

_____

5. In fact, this may be the (bad) storm of the year!

_____

CRITICAL THINKING

Explain why the sentence below is incorrect. Rewrite it correctly.

Yesterday, I felt the goodest that I have felt all week.

_____

_____

▶ 10.6 Spelling Adjectives Correctly   Exercise 77

Some one-syllable adjectives end with a vowel and a consonant.
Double the final consonant before you add *-er* or *-est*. Some
adjectives end in a consonant followed by a *y*. Change the *y*
to *i* before adding *-er* or *-est*.

Adjective	Comparative	Superlative
thin	thinner	thinnest
heavy	heavier	heaviest

**Write each sentence. Use the correct form of the adjective
in parentheses.**

1. This is the (pretty) bowl of all.

_____

2. These apples are (red) than most apples I have seen lately.

_____

3. Some of these oranges are (big) than grapefruits.

_____

4. These peaches are (juicy) than the ones we had last week.

_____

5. Eating more fruit can help you be (healthy) than you are now.

_____

CRITICAL THINKING

Rewrite the sentence below. Correct any mistakes in spelling.

California weather is dryest in the summer.

_____

10.7 Specific Adjectives   Exercise 78

> Some adjectives are more specific than other adjectives. You can make your writing clearer and more interesting by using specific adjectives to describe nouns or pronouns. The second sentence below uses more specific adjectives than the first.
>
> I wrote a <u>short</u> report about a <u>good</u> book.
> I wrote a <u>one-page</u> report about a <u>humorous</u> book.

Rewrite each sentence. Add specific adjectives to describe the underlined nouns.

1. The <u>students</u> waited for the <u>bus</u>.

_____

2. The <u>gust</u> of wind blew Henry's <u>umbrella</u>.

_____

3. <u>Raindrops</u> fell from the <u>cloud</u>.

_____

4. The rain soaked Henry's <u>coat</u> and <u>shoes</u>.

_____

5. The <u>bus</u> finally drove down the <u>street</u>.

_____

CRITICAL THINKING

The word *big* is an adjective. However, it is not very specific. Explain why it is not specific. Then list two specific adjectives that could replace the word *big*.

_____

_____

_____

Name _____ Date _____

 ## 10.8 Writing: Using Adjectives in Sentences

Adjectives can make your writing clearer and more interesting.

Follow the READ, PLAN, WRITE, and CHECK steps to write sentences with specific adjectives. The tips below will help you PLAN your writing.

PLAN   **Gather your ideas and organize them.**

- The questions in the assignments will help you gather your ideas.

- Use a Venn diagram to organize your ideas.

Complete the writing assignments below.

1. Write two sentences comparing life in the city to life in the country. What would be different? What would be the same? Use at least one comparative adjective.

_____

_____

_____

2. Write two sentences comparing life in a warm climate to life in a cold climate. What would be different? What would be the same? Use at least one comparative adjective.

_____

_____

_____

PUTTING IT ALL TOGETHER

How does the place where you live affect the kinds of things you do? On a separate sheet of paper, write a paragraph that compares types of places that people live. You may wish to use the sentences you wrote above. Add other sentences to make your ideas clearer.

Name ___Anthony F.___ Date _____

> An **adverb** tells more about a verb, verb phrase, adjective, or another adverb. An adverb tells *how, where, when,* or *how many times* an action takes place.
>
> He packed the box <u>quickly</u>. (tells *how*)
> He packed the box <u>here</u>. (tells *where*)
> <u>Today</u>, he packed the box. (tells *when*)
> He packed the box <u>once</u>. (tells *how many times*)

Write the adverb in each sentence. Then write how it is used in the sentence: *how, where, when,* **or** *how many times.*

1. Jeff bought his sister a birthday gift <u>yesterday</u>. _____

2. He quickly wrapped it in purple wrapping paper. _____

3. Gently, Jeff put the gift in a mailing box. _____

4. He carefully taped the box. _____

5. Then he looked for a pen on his desk. _____

6. Jeff neatly wrote his sister's address on the box. _____

7. Jeff looked at his watch twice to check the time. _____

8. The post office closes promptly at 5:00! _____

9. He walked quickly to the post office. _____

10. Jeff arrived there in time and mailed his sister's gift. _____

CRITICAL THINKING

You have started a new job. Write a sentence about your first day. Use an adverb. Next to the sentence, write how the adverb is used in the sentence.

_____

_____

Name _____ Date _____

11.2 Adverbs That Tell More About Adjectives

> Some adverbs tell more about adjectives. They tell *to what degree*.
>
> That movie was <u>very</u> exciting. (tells *how exciting the movie was*)
> The story was <u>especially</u> interesting. (tells *how interesting the story was*)

Write the adverb in each sentence. Then write the adjective that it tells more about.

1. Movie tickets have become <u>too</u> expensive. _*too how*_

2. We stood in a very <u>long</u> line to buy snacks. _*how was*_

3. The movie theater was almost <u>full</u>. _*how full*_

4. This theater has really <u>large</u> movie screens. _*large*_

5. It also has extremely <u>comfortable</u> chairs. _*how*_

6. The audience was especially <u>quiet</u>. _*how quiet*_

7. The music was <u>unusually</u> loud. _*what*_

8. The special effects were truly <u>amazing</u>. _*how amazing*_

9. I was somewhat sorry when the movie was <u>over</u>. _____

10. We were truly surprised by the ending. _____

CRITICAL THINKING

Write a sentence of your own. Use one of these adjectives:
scary, late, quiet, exciting. **Add an adverb that tells more about the adjective you used.**

_____

_____

_____

11.3 Adverbs That Tell More About Other Adverbs

> Some adverbs tell more about other adverbs. They tell *to what degree*. In the example below, the adverbs are underlined. The adverb that tells more about the other adverb is underlined twice.
>
> These black shoes fit <u>really</u> <u>well</u>. (*really* tells *how well*)

Each sentence contains two adverbs. Draw a line under each adverb. Draw a second line under the adverb that tells more about the other adverb.

1. I applied <u>extremely</u> early for a summer job this year.

2. If you wait <u>until</u> summertime, too often the good jobs are taken.

3. I am waiting <u>rather</u> eagerly for the store manager to call me.

4. I talked <u>somewhat</u> nervously in my first interview.

5. However, I think the interview went <u>fairly</u> well.

6. The <u>manager</u> called somewhat late this afternoon.

7. I listened <u>extremely</u> carefully to what she had to say.

8. She <u>very</u> cheerfully offered me a sales clerk job.

CRITICAL THINKING

Read the two sentences below. Write the one that uses the adverb *really* to describe another adverb. Then explain how you decided on your answer.

This car drives really well.   This car looks really shiny.

I do not fuckin
know.

▶ 11.4 Knowing When to Use Adjectives and Adverbs

Exercise 83

> Use adjectives to tell more about nouns and pronouns. Use adverbs to tell more about verbs, adjectives, and other adverbs. *Good* is an adjective. *Well* is an adverb.
>
> The bus was <u>late</u>. (tells more about the noun *bus*)
> The bus turned <u>slowly</u>. (tells more about the verb *turned)*
> The bus was <u>so</u> hot. (tells more about the adjective *hot*)
> The bus stopped <u>too</u> fast. (tells more about the adverb *fast*)
> I sat next to my <u>good</u> friend. (tells more about the noun *friend*)
> The bus driver drove <u>well</u>. (tells more about the verb *drove*)

Circle the correct word in parentheses. Write whether it is an adverb or an adjective.

1. The fog was very (thick, thickly) this morning. _____ *thick*

2. The (noisy, noisily) bus pulled to a stop. _____ *noisy*

3. We climbed up the (narrow, narrowly) steps. _____ *narrow*

4. I (quickly, quick) took a seat in the front of the bus. _____ *quickly*

5. It was hard to see (good, well) in the fog. _____ *well*

6. The bus driver drove very (slowly, slow). _____ *slow*

7. We arrived (safely, safe) at the mall. _____ *safely*

8. I saw my (good, well) friend in the music store. _____ *good*

CRITICAL THINKING

Explain why the sentence below is written incorrectly. Then write it correctly.

The sun shone warmly and bright.

_____ *The sun shined warmly & bright.*

▶ 11.5 Using Adverbs to Make Comparisons   Exercise 84

An adverb helps compare actions. To compare two actions, use an *-er* ending with some short adverbs. Use *more* or *less* before most adverbs. To compare more than two actions, use an *-est* ending with short adverbs. Use *most* or *least* with longer adverbs. Use *better* when comparing two things. Use *best* when comparing three or more things.

She speaks <u>faster</u> than her sister.
She speaks <u>less confidently</u> than I do.
He swims the <u>fastest</u> of the whole team.
He swims the <u>most powerfully</u> of all the team members.
He sings <u>better</u> than she does.
Our school choir sang the <u>best</u> of all the groups.

Circle the correct form of the adverb in parentheses.

1. Karl types (quicklier, more quickly) than I do.

2. If I practice, I will type (better, best) than I do now.

3. Joy types the (fastest, most fast) in our class.

4. This report took (longer, more long) to write than the other one did.

5. I work (less, least) quickly than you do.

6. Which of these three titles do you like (better, best)?

7. I need to proofread my report (more carefully, carefullier).

8. I type better when I sit (closer, more close) to the keyboard.

9. I draw (better, more well) on the computer than I type.

10. I draw the (more skillfully, most skillfully) of all my friends.

CRITICAL THINKING

Write a sentence to compare two movies, books, or TV shows.
Use at least one adverb.

_____

▶ 11.6 Using Negatives Correctly   Exercise 85

> A **negative** is a word or phrase that means "no." Some negative
> words are *nobody*, *none*, *nothing*, and *not*. Avoid using double negatives.
>
> Incorrect: Scarcely nobody was in the movie theater.
> Correct: Scarcely anybody was in the movie theater.

Write each sentence correctly. Use only one negative word.

1. Scarcely no one likes the same movies I do.

_____

2. Hardly nobody wants to go to the movies with me.

_____

3. I have not seen none of the new movies.

_____

4. Neither of my best friends never offers to go with me.

_____

5. They cannot never expect me to wait for them.

_____

6. When my friends pick the movie, I barely never like it.

_____

CRITICAL THINKING

**Explain why the sentence below is written incorrectly. Then
write it correctly.**

I hardly do nothing except my homework after school.

_____

_____

▶ 11.6 Using Contractions Correctly   **Exercise 86**

A **contraction** is a shortened form of two or more words. *Not* can be joined to a verb to form a contraction. When a contraction includes *not,* do not use another negative word in the sentence.

Incorrect: I didn't see nothing in the box.
Correct: I didn't see anything in the box.

**Rewrite each sentence correctly. Use only one negative word.
If a sentence is correct, write** *correct.*

1. Jacob wasn't at neither of the meetings.

_____

2. Didn't no one tell him about the meetings?

_____

3. Couldn't none of you find him?

_____

4. I can't find him anywhere.

_____

5. Nobody hasn't seen him today.

_____

CRITICAL THINKING

**Explain why the sentence below is written incorrectly.
Then write it correctly.**

I haven't never met Susan.

_____

_____

▶ 11.7 Specific Adverbs   Exercise 87

Using specific adverbs can make your writing clearer and more interesting. The second sentence below uses more specific adverbs.

Karl spoke <u>well</u>.
Karl spoke <u>clearly</u> and <u>confidently</u>.

Circle the more specific adverb in parentheses.

1. Kenya and I are (especially, very) good friends.

2. I wanted to throw Kenya a (big, magnificent) party.

3. Bryce helped me write the invitations (nicely, neatly).

4. Ama's decorations were (nice, beautiful).

5. Lionel greeted our friends (warmly, well) as they arrived.

6. He set the gifts (easily, gently) on a table.

7. The guest waited (nicely, patiently) for her to arrive.

8. We all yelled (wildly, loudly) when she walked into the room.

9. Everyone greeted Kenya (kindly, lovingly).

10. Her smile was (bright, sparkling).

11. She (happily, excitedly) opened the gifts.

12. The party was (very, extremely) exciting.

CRITICAL THINKING

Write a sentence about one task that you did yesterday.
Use at least one specific adverb.

_____

_____

Name _____ Date _____

Using specific adverbs helps make your writing clearer and more interesting.

Follow the READ, PLAN, WRITE, and CHECK steps to write sentences with specific adverbs. The tips below will help you PLAN your writing.

PLAN   **Gather your ideas and organize them.**

- The questions in the assignments will help you gather your ideas.
- Use a spider map to organize your ideas.

Complete the writing assignments below.

1. You are at a sporting event or watching one on TV. Write two sentences that describe what is happening. What is the action? Who is playing? What is the score? Use specific adverbs.

_____

_____

_____

2. Write two other sentences that describe what you are doing while you watch the event. Where are you? Who are you with? Use specific adverbs.

_____

_____

_____

PUTTING IT ALL TOGETHER

Why do millions of people enjoy watching sporting events? On a separate sheet of paper, write a paragraph about a sporting event that you have watched. You may wish to use the sentences you have written above. Add other sentences to connect these sentences and to explain your ideas.

Name _____ Date _____

12.1 What Is a Preposition?   Exercise 89

A **preposition** shows how a noun or pronoun is related to another word or group of words in a sentence. The prepositions are underlined in the examples below.

We went <u>to</u> the library.
I looked <u>for</u> books <u>about</u> Colorado.

Write the preposition in each sentence. Some sentences have more than one preposition.

1. School will be out for the summer in two weeks. _____

2. I will enjoy sleeping late in the mornings. _____

3. I will play basketball with my friends every day. _____

4. Everyone except Tim is on the team at school. _____

5. The park down the street has a basketball court. _____

6. When it gets hot, we go to the pool at Tim's house. _____

7. Todd can swim across the whole pool underwater. _____

8. Everyone around the pool watches him. _____

9. He swims so far underneath the water. _____

10. We do many things during our summer break. _____

CRITICAL THINKING

Add two different prepositions to the sentences below. Then explain how the prepositions change the meaning of the sentence.

I walked _____ the fence.   I walked _____ the fence.

_____

_____

▶ 12.2 What Is a Prepositional Phrase?   Exercise 90

> A **prepositional phrase** is a group of words that begins with a
> preposition and ends with a noun or pronoun. The noun or
> pronoun at the end of the phrase is the **object of the preposition.**
> There may be other words between the preposition and the object.
> In the example below, the preposition is underlined once. The
> object of the preposition is underlined twice.
>
>   She drove <u>down</u> the <u>street</u>.

**Write the prepositional phrase or phrases in each sentence.
Draw one line under each preposition. Draw two lines under
each object of the preposition.**

1. In 1948, Mother Teresa began helping the poor. _____

2. She trained at a hospital. _____

3. Then she opened a medical center among the poor. _____

4. Mother Teresa also opened a school for poor children. _____

5. Other nuns lived and worked with Mother Teresa. _____

6. She became well-known for her charity work. _____

7. She helped many people during her lifetime. _____

8. Over the years, she received many awards. _____

9. In 1979, she won the Nobel Peace Prize. _____

10. At 87 years of age, Mother Teresa died. _____

CRITICAL THINKING

**Write two sentences that describe where you are sitting right
now. Use two prepositional phrases in your sentences.**

_____

_____

Name _____ Date _____

The object of a preposition can be a pronoun. The personal pronouns in the box can be used as objects of the preposition.

Personal Pronouns						
me	you	her	him	it	us	them

Add a personal pronoun of your own to complete each sentence.

1. Mr. Osborn asked us to do some work for _____him_____ today.

2. His house needs repairs made to _____It_____ before winter.

3. Harlee handed the paintbrush to _____me_____.

4. The paintbrush had too much paint on _____It_____.

5. It dripped paint all over both of _____us_____.

6. Harlee worked with _____them_____ on the door.

7. As Ken washed the windows, Jill worked beside _____me_____.

8. Marie stood on a ladder by _____me_____.

9. Below _____her_____, there was a bucket of paint.

10. As she stepped off the ladder, she almost fell into _____them_____!

CRITICAL THINKING

Rewrite the sentence below. Replace the underlined word with a personal pronoun.

I will go to the movies with <u>Greg</u> later today.

_____

_____

12.4 Using Correct Verb Forms After Prepositional Phrases

Sometimes, a prepositional phrase comes after the main noun
or pronoun in the subject. The verb or verb phrase of the
sentence still must agree with the main noun or pronoun. The
verb does not need to agree with the noun or pronoun in the
prepositional phrase.

The young people work hard.

The young people in the band work hard.

Write the correct verb form in parentheses.

1. The members of the committee (works, work) together. _____ work

2. One of them (run, runs) the meetings. _____ runs

3. Many on the committee (attend, attends) every meeting. _____ attend

4. Two people in the group (is, are) in charge. _____ are

5. The tables in the meeting room (form, forms) a circle. _____ form

6. One of the members always (take, takes) notes. _____ take

7. My notes from the last meeting (look, looks) messy. _____ looks

8. The subject of the meetings (is, are) a new building plan. _____ are

9. Mark's ideas about the building (sound, sounds) great. _____ sounds

10. The next two meetings about the plan (start, starts) at 8:00. _____ starts

CRITICAL THINKING

**The verb phrase in the sentence below does not agree with the
subject. Tell what the correct verb should be, and explain why.**

The questions on this test is very easy.

_____

_____

Name _Anthony_   Date _____

▶ 12.5 Using Prepositions Correctly   Exercise 93

> Use the preposition *between* when you refer to two people, things, or groups. Use the preposition *among* when you refer to three or more people, things, or groups. Use the preposition *beside* when you mean "next to." Use the preposition *besides* when you mean "in addition to" or "except."
>
>   I cannot decide <u>between these two shirts</u>.
>   I cannot decide <u>among all the shoes</u>.
>   Christopher put his baseball <u>beside his glove</u>.
>   <u>Besides the ball</u>, he brought his bat and glove to practice.

Write the correct preposition for each sentence.

1. We will not go anywhere (beside, **besides**) the mountains. _besides_

2. We will rent a cabin (**between**, among) the pine trees. _between_

3. (Beside, **Besides**) our family, two others will be there. _besides_

4. We had to choose (between, **among**) six cabins. _between_

5. The cabins are (**beside**, besides) a stream. _beside_

6. Our cabin is (**between**, among) the other two cabins. _between_

7. It will be fun to be (between, **among**) friends. _among_

8. Can anyone (beside, **besides**) me pack this suitcase? _besides_

9. I will sit (**beside**, besides) the window so I can see. _beside_

10. You can sit (**between**, among) Jason and Carol. _between_

CRITICAL THINKING

Write two sentences using the words *beside* and *besides*.

_____

_____

_____

Name _____ Date _____

A preposition shows how a noun or a pronoun is related to another word in a sentence. It also gives more information in a sentence.

Follow the READ, PLAN, WRITE, and CHECK steps to write sentences with prepositional phrases. The tips below will help you PLAN your writing.

PLAN 　 **Gather your ideas and organize them.**

- The questions in the assignments will help you gather your ideas.
- Draw a sketch of your ideas.

Complete the writing assignments below.

1. Your city has asked for ideas about a new park that is being built. In what part of your community should the park be built? Write two sentences describing where you would like the park to be. Use at least two prepositional phrases.

_____

_____

_____

2. Write two sentences that describe what you would like the park to look like. What things would you like in the park? How would you like the park to be arranged? Use at least two prepositional phrases.

_____

_____

_____

PUTTING IT ALL TOGETHER

What are the benefits of building parks? On a separate sheet of paper, write a paragraph describing a new park for your community. You may wish to use the sentences you have written above. Add other sentences to make your ideas clearer.

13.1 Appositives and Appositive Phrases

> An **appositive** is a noun that follows another noun or pronoun to tell more about it. An **appositive phrase** is a group of words that includes an appositive. Appositives and appositive phrases are usually set off from the rest of the sentence by commas.
>
> Our coach, <u>Mr. Scott</u>, talked to the team. (appositive)
> I saw Ed, <u>a friend of mine</u>, yesterday. (appositive phrase)

Draw a line under the appositive or appositive phrase in each sentence.

1. Mrs. Stevens, my English teacher, took our class to the library.

2. I returned the book, *Tony's World*, that I checked out last week.

3. I went to find a science fiction book, my favorite kind.

4. The librarian, Mr. Clark, helped me find a book.

5. I checked out *Tomorrow Land*, a new science fiction book.

6. It was written by Brian Riggs, my favorite author.

7. I will use it to do my homework, a short book report.

8. The librarian, Mrs. Mills, said the book was due back on March 2.

9. Nancy, the first person in line, checked out a book about music.

10. *Hear the Beat*, the book she chose, is 72 pages long.

CRITICAL THINKING

Write a sentence of your own about someone in your family. Use an appositive phrase.

_____

_____

Name _____ Date _____

▶ 13.2 Participles and Participial Phrases Exercise 96

A **participle** is a verb that is used as an adjective. A **participial phrase** begins with a present participle or a past participle. It gives more information about a noun or pronoun.

The <u>folded</u> towels are sitting on the shelf. (participle)
<u>Running out the door</u>, I forgot my coat. (participial phrase)
<u>Stopped at a light</u>, I saw you. (participial phrase)

Draw a line under the participial phrase in each sentence.

1. Remembering my homework, I gathered my books.

2. Walking quickly, I headed for the library.

3. My notebook, packed in my book bag, was heavy.

4. Other students, whispering quietly, sat at the tables.

5. Thinking about my report, I tried to choose a topic.

6. The librarian, noticing me, asked if I needed help.

7. Shaking my head, I said, "No thanks."

8. I found a book written by my favorite author.

9. Taking notes, I skimmed through the pages.

10. Finished with my report, I finally went home.

CRITICAL THINKING

Circle the sentence that has a participial phrase. Explain how you know that the underlined part is a participial phrase.

<u>Thinking carefully</u>, I wrote the answer.

<u>Happy with my topic</u>, I started to write.

_____

_____

Name _____ Date _____

You can use a participial phrase to combine sentences. The sentences below were combined using the underlined participial phrase. A comma is used to separate the participial phrase from the rest of the sentence.

Kevin worked quickly. Kevin finished before anyone else.
<u>Working quickly</u>, Kevin finished before anyone else.

Combine each pair of sentences below. Use a participial phrase. Use a comma to separate the participial phrase from the rest of the sentence.

1. Juan was training for a new job. Juan listened to his boss.

_____

2. His boss talked slowly. His boss explained how to take an order.

_____

3. Juan waited on a customer. Juan took an order.

_____

4. His boss checked the order. She nodded her head.

_____

5. She smiled. She told Juan that he had done a good job.

_____

CRITICAL THINKING

Write a sentence of your own about how you study for a test. Use a participial phrase.

_____

_____

13.3 Gerunds and Gerund Phrases

Exercise 98

A **gerund** is a verb that is used as a noun. It ends in *-ing*.
A **gerund phrase** begins with a gerund and has other words that add to its meaning.

    <u>Sleeping</u> is important to your health. (gerund)
    <u>Eating good food</u> helps you stay healthy. (gerund phrase)

Draw a line under the gerund or gerund phrase in each sentence.

1. Swimming is my favorite kind of exercise.

2. I practice swimming laps across the pool.

3. The part I like best is being outside in the sun.

4. I also enjoy writing stories.

5. When I write, thinking of a title is easy for me.

6. Writing the first paragraph is more difficult.

7. I try to avoid using short sentences in my writing.

8. I often enjoy writing about my friends.

9. Reading my stories to my friends can be fun.

10. You can make more friends by being helpful to others.

11. You can lose friends by talking about other people.

12. Trying your best is a way to earn respect from others.

CRITICAL THINKING

Rewrite the sentence below so that it has a gerund phrase.

To do your best is the key to success.

_____

Name _____ Date _____

▶ 13.4 Infinitives and Infinitive Phrases   Exercise 99

An **infinitive** is made up of the word *to* plus the plural form of a verb. An **infinitive phrase** begins with an infinitive. Infinitives and infinitive phrases can be used as nouns, adjectives, or adverbs.

> She tried <u>to tell me her name</u>. (used as a noun)
> It was a good time <u>to leave</u>. (used as an adjective)
> He hurried <u>to get home</u>. (used as an adverb)

Write the infinitive phrase in each sentence.

1. Josh likes to play the guitar. _____

2. Josh wanted to attend a concert. _____

3. He needed to earn money for his ticket. _____

4. To buy a ticket costs twelve dollars. _____

5. A neighbor offered Josh six dollars to mow his lawn. _____

6. Josh quickly agreed to do the work. _____

7. His mom paid him four dollars to wash her car. _____

8. He asked his sister to lend him two dollars. _____

9. She agreed to give him the money. _____

10. Now Josh can buy a ticket to see the concert. _____

CRITICAL THINKING

Circle the sentence below that has an infinitive. Explain how you can tell if the underlined part is an infinitive.

Jennifer went <u>to the store</u>.

Ken asked her <u>to buy some bread</u>.

_____

_____

Name_____ Date_____

 13.5 Writing: Using Phrases in Sentences   **Exercise 100**

A phrase is a group of words that completes an idea. It does not contain both a subject and a verb. Appositives, participles, gerunds, and infinitives are all kinds of phrases.

Follow the READ, PLAN, WRITE, and CHECK steps to write sentences that contain phrases. The tips below will help you PLAN your writing.

PLAN   **Gather your ideas and organize them.**

- The questions in the assignments will help you gather your ideas.

- Use an outline to organize your ideas.

Complete the writing assignments below.

1. If you could learn about anything, what would it be? Write two sentences that tell what you would like to learn. Explain why you would like to learn this skill or topic. Use at least one infinitive and one gerund in your sentences.

_____

_____

_____

2. What could you do to learn this skill or topic? Write two sentences that tell what steps you could take to learn more about this skill or topic. Use at least one participial phrase and one appositive phrase in your sentences.

_____

_____

_____

PUTTING IT ALL TOGETHER

Why is it important to learn new things? On a separate sheet of paper, write a paragraph about something you would like to learn. You may wish to use the sentences you have written above. Add other sentences to explain your ideas.

Name _____ Date _____

> A **simple sentence** expresses *one* complete thought. It often has one subject and one predicate. A simple sentence can also have a **compound subject**, a **compound predicate**, or both. In the examples below, the subjects are underlined once. The verbs in the predicates are underlined twice.
>
>   Jill types letters. (one subject and one predicate)
>   Ron and Jen work in the mailroom. (compound subject)
>   Marc writes and files memos. (compound predicate)
>   Jeremy and Katelyn answer the phone and take messages.
>   (compound subject and compound predicate)

Write whether each sentence has a compound subject, a compound predicate, or both.

1. Isabel and Anthony take music lessons. _____

2. Isabel sings and plays the keyboard. _____

3. Anthony writes songs and plays the drums. _____

4. Isabel and Anthony play at parties on weekends. _____

5. Chris and Greg set up the equipment and check the sound. _____

CRITICAL THINKING

Answer each question. Use simple sentences.

1. Who are your best friends? Use a compound subject. _____

   _____

2. What do your friends do for fun? Use a compound predicate. _____

   _____

3. What do you and a friend do together for fun? Use a compound

   subject and a compound predicate. _____

   _____

14.2 Coordinating Conjunctions

Exercise 102

A **coordinating conjunction** joins words, phrases, and sentences.

Coordinating Conjunctions						
and	but	or	nor	for	so	yet

Jim <u>and</u> Laura (joins words)
a nice dinner <u>or</u> a boring movie (joins phrases)
The movie was boring, <u>so</u> we went home. (joins sentences)

Draw a line under the coordinating conjunction in each sentence.

1. Bill and Latisha took a taxi to the airport.

2. They left late, yet they arrived in plenty of time.

3. They walked quickly, so they would not miss their plane.

4. They carried one bag with them, for they were staying two days.

5. The plane was at the gate, but passengers waited to board.

6. Neither the pilot nor the crew had arrived.

7. Finally, passengers boarded the plane and sat down.

8. The plane landed safely, and the passengers clapped.

CRITICAL THINKING

Compare the two groups of sentences below. Tell which group of sentences sounds better, and why.

1. Jill ate chicken. Jill ate salad. She was still hungry.

2. Jill ate chicken and salad, but she was still hungry.

_____

_____

_____

▶ 14.3 Compound Sentences   Exercise 103

> A **compound sentence** is made up of two or more independent clauses. An **independent clause** forms a complete sentence. Coordinating conjunctions often join the independent clauses in a compound sentence. In the compound sentence below, the subjects are underlined once. The verbs are underlined twice.
>
> <u>Jeff</u> <u>cooked</u> dinner, and <u>Marcia</u> <u>washed</u> the dishes.

Write *Compound* if a sentence is a compound sentence.
Write *Simple* if a sentence is a simple sentence.

1. Many dogs and cats have lived in the White House, but some

unusual pets have also lived there. _____

2. Abraham Lincoln spared the life of a Thanksgiving turkey, and it

became a family pet. _____

3. President Theodore Roosevelt's children kept snakes as pets in

the White House. _____

4. A cow belonging to William Howard Taft grazed on the White

House lawn and was called Pauline Wayne. _____

5. A raccoon named Rebecca was often seen splashing in a White

House tub, for she was Calvin Coolidge's pet. _____

6. John Kennedy's daughter had a pony, and she rode it on the

grounds of the White House. _____

CRITICAL THINKING

Read the sentence below. Is it a compound sentence or a simple sentence? Explain how you decided on your answer.

Jamie thinks skateboarding is fun, but I like in-line skating better.

_____

_____

▶ 14.4 Commas in Compound Sentences   Exercise 104

> Use a comma before the coordinating conjunction in a
> compound sentence.
>
> Sal is learning French, but Nancy is learning Spanish.
> Laura is staying late for band practice, so I will pick up Kim.

Add a comma in each sentence where it is needed.

1. People have busy lives and many do not make time to exercise.

2. Exercising is fun and it keeps you in good shape.

3. You can go to a health club or you can workout at home.

4. Some people play team sports but others exercise on their own.

5. Exercise builds strong muscles and it also makes bones strong.

6. Kickboxing is great exercise yet some people think it is too difficult.

7. Too much exercise can make you tired so try not to overdo it.

8. Exercise is important but people need to eat well too.

9. Eat fruits and vegetables so your body can fight off sicknesses.

10. Eat a low-fat diet for it also helps keep you healthy.

11. Exercise a few times a week and your body will thank you!

12. Are you exercising often and eating well and are you getting a good
    night's rest and taking vitamins?

CRITICAL THINKING

**Do you think commas before coordinating conjunctions in
compound sentences make sentences easier to understand?
Explain why or why not.**

_____

_____

Name _____   Date _____

14.5 Using Coordinating Conjunctions to Combine Sentences

Exercise 105

> To form a compound sentence, combine two simple sentences.
> Use a coordinating conjunction and a comma to combine them.
>
> Akia draws pictures by hand. Ed uses a computer.
> Akia draws pictures by hand, but Ed uses a computer.

Combine each pair of sentences. Use a coordinating conjunction and a comma.

1. Sybil had saved some money from her part-time job.

She wanted to open a bank account. _____

_____

2. A savings account would earn her money interest.

The interest rates were very low. _____

_____

3. She also needed to pay some bills.

She had to be able to write checks. _____

_____

4. Sybil decided to open a checking account.

A bank officer helped her apply for the account. _____

_____

CRITICAL THINKING

Write a simple sentence about one of your favorite foods.
Write another simple sentence about a food you do not like.
Combine the two sentences to make a compound sentence.

Simple sentence: _____

Simple sentence: _____

Compound sentence: _____

14.6 Avoiding Run-On Sentences Exercise 106

A **run-on sentence** is made up of two or more sentences that are written as one sentence. To correct a run-on sentence, you can divide it into two simple sentences. You also can add a comma and a coordinating conjunction or use a semicolon.

Jan took the bus it was crowded. (run-on sentence)
Jan took the bus. It was crowded. (two simple sentences)
Jan took the bus, and it was crowded. (comma and coordinating conjunction)
Jan took the bus; it was crowded. (semicolon)

Write each run-on sentence correctly. Add a coordinating conjunction and comma to correct each sentence.

1. Gail baby-sits after school she loves children.

   _____

2. Dan mows lawns the money will help pay for his car.

   _____

3. Roy's bike is broken he can use mine to deliver papers.

   _____

Add a semicolon to correct each run-on sentence.

4. Tornadoes are terrible storms they kill hundreds each year.

5. The Midwest gets a lot of tornadoes it is called Tornado Alley.

6. Weather reports warn us about tornadoes take cover if a tornado is seen in your area.

CRITICAL THINKING

Why is it important to avoid run-on sentences?

_____

_____

▶ 14.7 Writing Compound Sentences   Exercise 107

Good writing has simple and compound sentences.

Follow the READ, PLAN, WRITE, and CHECK steps to form compound sentences. The tips below will help you PLAN your writing.

PLAN   **Gather your ideas and organize them.**

• Read the assignments and discuss your ideas with a partner.

• Use an outline to organize your ideas.

Complete the writing assignments below.

1. You have decided to clean up several places in your neighborhood. Write a compound sentence about two places you will clean up. Write a second compound sentence about what type of work you expect to do in each place.

_____

_____

_____

2. Write a compound sentence about what you could do to keep people from littering in the places you have cleaned. Then write a compound sentence that explains why people should not litter.

_____

_____

_____

PUTTING IT ALL TOGETHER

Why is it important to have clean communities? On a separate sheet of paper, write a paragraph that explains what you could do to help keep your community clean. Explain why it is important for people to keep their communities clean. Include at least two compound sentences in your paragraph. You may wish to use the sentences you have written above. Add other sentences to explain your ideas.

15.1 Subordinating Conjunctions

> A **subordinating conjunction** begins a **dependent clause**.
> A dependent clause cannot stand alone as a complete sentence.
> In each example below, the dependent clause is underlined once.
> The subordinating conjunction is underlined twice.
>
>   I must study <u><u>because</u> I have a test tomorrow</u>.
>
>   <u><u>If</u> you want</u>, we can study together.

Draw one line under the dependent clause in each sentence.
Draw two lines under the subordinating conjunction.

1. You must follow many rules when you drive.

2. If the light is red, you must stop.

3. Do not go until the light turns green.

4. Slow down whenever you see a yellow light.

5. While a school bus is flashing its red lights, you must wait.

6. Although no cars are coming, always stop at a stop sign.

7. Use your signal before you turn or change lanes.

8. Always check your mirrors so that you can see other cars.

9. Always wear a seat belt because it could save your life.

10. Pull over when you see flashing lights on a fire truck.

CRITICAL THINKING

When do you need to use a comma with a dependent clause?
(Hint: Look at the practice sentences above for a clue.)

_____

_____

_____

15.2 Adverb Clauses in Complex Sentences

> An **adverb clause** is a dependent clause that begins with a subordinating conjunction. The clause acts as an adverb. It tells more about a verb, an adjective, or another adverb. The adverb clauses are underlined in the examples below.
>
> The radio will not work <u>because it is broken</u>. (tells *why*)
> It broke <u>when it fell on the floor</u>. (tells *when*)
> Tom looked at it <u>as if he knew how to fix it</u>. (tells *how*)
> I like to shop <u>wherever CDs are sold</u>. (tells *where*)

Draw a line under the adverb clause in each sentence. Then write which question it answers: *why, when, how,* **or** *where.*

1. This movie seems as though it will last forever. _____

2. I feel as if I could fall asleep. _____

3. I always get cold when I go to the movies. _____

4. Maci brought a sweater so that she would be warm. _____

5. The theater should not be cold since it is so hot outside. _____

6. I am going outside because I am too cold. _____

7. I want to sit where the sun is shining. _____

8. You can sit wherever you want. _____

9. I will feel better after I warm up. _____

10. Let us go back in the theater before the movie is over. _____

CRITICAL THINKING

Rewrite the sentence below. Replace the underlined adverb with an adverb clause.

I will call you <u>soon</u>. _____

_____

Name _____ Date _____

15.2 Using Commas in Complex Sentences   Exercise 110

A **complex sentence** has an independent clause and a dependent clause. Put a comma after the dependent clause if it comes before the independent clause. In the examples below, the dependent clauses are underlined. Notice which sentence has a comma.

You will not get wet <u>as long as you have an umbrella</u>.
<u>As long as you have an umbrella</u>, you will not get wet.

Write each sentence. Add commas where they are needed. If the sentence is correct, write *correct*.

1. Because I need to do some research I am going to the library.

_____

2. Because my report is due tomorrow I must go today.

_____

3. I will leave after I finish breakfast.

_____

4. I can stay until the library closes at 9:00.

_____

5. Before I turn in my report I will make a copy of it.

_____

CRITICAL THINKING

The sentence below has two mistakes. Explain why the sentence is incorrect. Then write it correctly.

Although it is late I will stay up, until I finish my homework.

_____

_____

15.3 Using Adverb Clauses to Combine Sentences

> You can use an adverb clause to combine sentences. The adverb
> clause can go at the beginning or the end of the sentence. A
> subordinating conjunction is used to form the adverb clause.
> Notice how the sentences were combined in the examples below.
> The subordinating conjunction is underlined.
>
> Ray mowed the lawn. The grass was very long.
> Ray mowed the lawn <u>because</u> the grass was very long.
> <u>Because</u> the grass was very long, Ray mowed the lawn.

**Combine each pair of sentences. Use an adverb clause. Draw a
line under each subordinating conjunction. Remember to use
commas as needed.**

1. Michael loves bicycle racing. It is so exciting.

   _____

2. He has some spare time. He trains on his bike.

   _____

3. He wants to enter a race. He gets really good at riding.

   _____

4. Michael must train very hard. He can win a race.

   _____

5. Racing is very hard. It is also fun.

   _____

CRITICAL THINKING

Explain how using adverb clauses can improve your writing.

_____

_____

▶ 15.4 Identifying Adjective Clauses   Exercise 112

An **adjective clause** is a dependent clause that acts like an adjective in a sentence. An adjective clause tells more about a noun or pronoun. The words in the box are used to begin adjective clauses. In the example below, the adjective clause is underlined.

who	which	when	that
whose	whom	where	

There is the man <u>who gave the speech</u>.

Draw a line under the adjective clause in each sentence.

1. Here are the flowers that I planted last year.

2. I received them from a woman whose garden is always beautiful.

3. I do not know anyone who knows more about plants.

4. I need to find a book that will teach me more about gardening.

5. This is the spot where I will plant some roses.

6. The plants that need the most shade should be planted here.

7. Timothy brought me some plants that will bloom all summer.

8. The bird bath that I put in the garden is empty.

9. The birds need a place where they can drink and bathe.

10. Butterflies flock to the bush that is near the fence.

CRITICAL THINKING

How is an adjective clause different from an adverb clause?

_____

_____

_____

15.4 Using Commas with Adjective Clauses

> Some adjective clauses are not necessary to the meaning of a sentence. These adjective clauses are set apart from the rest of the sentence by commas. Other adjective clauses are necessary to the meaning of a sentence. Commas are *not* used when the clause is necessary. In the examples below, the adjective clauses are underlined.
>
> José, <u>who is my friend</u>, works here. (not necessary)
> He has a job <u>that pays very well</u>. (necessary)

Draw a line under the adjective clause in each sentence.
Add commas where they are needed. Some sentences may
not need commas.

1. The space shuttle which left last Monday will land tomorrow.

2. The astronauts who are on board will be glad to get home.

3. Their families who are at home will be waiting for them.

4. The astronauts eat packaged food that tastes pretty good.

5. One astronaut who is on the shuttle is 65 years old.

6. The area where the shuttle will land is deserted.

CRITICAL THINKING

Write an adjective clause of your own to complete each
sentence below.

1. That was the class _____.

2. This is the street _____.

3. Tuesday is the day _____.

4. Math is the subject _____.

5. My friends are the ones _____.

15.5 Using Adjective Clauses to Combine Sentences

Exercise 114

> You can use an adjective clause to combine sentences. Always write the adjective clause after the word it describes. Notice how the sentences were combined in the examples below. The adjective clause is underlined.
>
> The noise was very loud. The noise woke me up.
> The noise <u>that woke me up</u> was very loud.

Combine each pair of sentences. Use an adjective clause. Draw a line under the adjective clause. Remember to use commas when necessary.

1. The crowd waited for the concert. The concert started late.

_____

2. I saw many of my friends. My friends were at the concert.

_____

3. We had great seats. The seats were near the stage.

_____

4. The opening act was a band. I had never heard of that band.

_____

5. The last band played many songs. The band is my favorite group.

_____

CRITICAL THINKING

How can using adjective clauses improve your writing?

_____

_____

▶ 15.6 Noun Clauses   Exercise 115

> A **noun clause** is a dependent clause that is used as a noun in a
> sentence. It often answers the questions *who* or *what*. In the
> examples below, the noun clauses are underlined.
>
>   I do not know <u>what I did with my notebook</u>.
>   I think <u>that I gave it to someone</u>.
>   <u>Whoever borrowed my notes</u> must have my notebook.

Write the noun clause in each sentence.

1. I wonder what made these tracks. _____

2. Whatever it was must be very big. _____

3. Look at how big each footprint is! _____

4. I think that it must be some kind of bear. _____

5. You said that there were no wild animals here. _____

6. I did not know that there were any around here. _____

7. I cannot see where the tracks lead. _____

8. I am sure that it is far away now. _____

9. Let us hope that it is. _____

10. Maybe tomorrow we can find out what it was. _____

CRITICAL THINKING

Complete each sentence below with a noun clause of your own.

1. I wish _____.

2. _____ wins the game.

3. We may never know _____.

15.7 Writing Complex Sentences

> A complex sentence contains an independent clause and a dependent clause. Two kinds of dependent clauses are adverb clauses and adjective clauses.
>
> Follow the READ, PLAN, WRITE, and CHECK steps to write complex sentences with adverb and adjective clauses. The questions below will help you CHECK your writing.
>
> **CHECK   How can you improve your writing?**
>   - Do your sentences answer the assignment?
>   - Did you use adverb and adjective clauses correctly?
>   - How can you make your writing clearer?

Complete the writing assignments below.

1. What have been your two favorite classes? Write two complex sentences explaining why these classes were your favorite. Use adverb and adjective clauses in your sentences.

   _____

   _____

   _____

2. What have been your two least favorite classes? Write two complex sentences explaining why these classes were your least favorite. Use adverb and adjective clauses in your sentences.

   _____

   _____

   _____

PUTTING IT ALL TOGETHER

Why is it important to take different kinds of classes? On a separate sheet of paper, write a paragraph about which classes have been your favorite and which have been your least favorite. You may wish to use the sentences that you have written above. Add other sentences to connect your ideas.

▶ 16.1 What Is a Paragraph?   Exercise 117

A **paragraph** is a group of sentences that are placed together and relate to the same idea or topic. This topic is called the **main idea**. The main idea tells what the paragraph is about. All of the sentences in a paragraph must relate to the main idea. All of the sentences below relate to the main idea of the Blarney Stone.

The Blarney Stone is a large piece of limestone. It is found in Blarney Castle near Cork, Ireland. The stone was moved to the castle in 1146. Some people believe that anyone who kisses the stone will become a very good speaker. The word *blarney* now means "clever talk."

Write the main idea of each paragraph.

1. Many people around the world enjoy the sport of 10-pin bowling. Each year, more than 80 million Americans play this sport. Bowling is also popular in other countries, such as Canada and Japan.

_____

2. The black lines you see on a package at the supermarket are called a bar code. A computer reads the bar code. The bar code tells the computer what the product is. It also tells the computer how much the product costs. Bar codes were first used in 1973.

_____

3. The deer tick is a tiny insect. These ticks often live in wooded or grassy areas. A deer tick is so small that many people never know they have been bitten by one. Often, people who have been bitten by a deer tick develop a rash.

_____

CRITICAL THINKING

Why would it be difficult to read letters, articles, and stories if they were not written in paragraphs?

_____

_____

16.2 The Topic Sentence   Exercise 118

A **topic sentence** states the main idea of a paragraph. It lets the reader know what the paragraph is about. The topic sentence can be anywhere in the paragraph. The topic sentence is underlined in the example below.

Solar power uses the sun to make energy. Special panels are placed in the sunlight. These panels turn the sun into electricity. On cloudy days, the panels cannot make electricity because there is not enough sun. Therefore, solar power is not useful in some places.

Draw a line under the topic sentence of each paragraph below. The topic sentence can be anywhere in the paragraph.

1. Thomas Edison patented, or received the rights to, more inventions in his lifetime than any other American. He received his first patent when he was just 21 years old. Two of his most well-known inventions are the light bulb and the phonograph. He received 1,093 patents by the time he died.

2. A group of fish is called a school. A flock is a group of birds. A group of geese is called a gaggle. The name for a group of lions is a pride. Different groups of animals have special names.

3. The 4-H club began as a way for farm children to learn more about farming. Today, children who live in the city and in the country learn from the club's hands-on activities. The 4-H club helps all kinds of children get involved in their community.

4. If you are ever in a fire, you should follow these fire safety tips. If you smell smoke, get to the nearest exit. Check that the fire is not blocking your exit. Stay close to the ground so that you do not breathe smoke. Call for help when you have reached safety.

CRITICAL THINKING

Why is it important to have a topic sentence in a paragraph?

_____

_____

16.3 Supporting Details

Supporting details are the sentences that make up the body of a paragraph. They give more information about the topic sentence. They often answer the questions *who, what, where, when,* or *why.* In the example below, the supporting details are underlined.

Last night's basketball game was great. <u>At the end of the first half, the Jaguars were ahead by ten points.</u> <u>In the last minute, the game was tied.</u> <u>With five seconds to go, the Jaguars got the ball and scored to win the game.</u>

Draw a line under the supporting details in each paragraph below. The topic sentence is not always the first sentence.

1. Some worms are smaller than a grain of rice. On the other hand, one kind of worm found in Australia can grow to be 12 feet long. However, the longest worm ever found was in South Africa. It was over 20 feet long. Worms come in all sizes.

2. The city was in the middle of a heat wave. The temperature had been over 100 degrees for seven days in a row. There had been no rain to cool things off. Even at night, the temperature stayed in the 90s. So many people were using air conditioners and fans that the power kept going off.

3. Scientists in Massachusetts have invented "smell chips." These computer chips are filled with odors that can be released by TV signals. When you see a pizza on TV, you might smell pepperoni. If you see a rose, the smell of flowers would fill the air. In the future, we may be watching "smell-o-vision."

CRITICAL THINKING

Cross out the sentence that does NOT support the topic sentence in the paragraph below. Explain why it does not belong.

Nick hoped he would be chosen for the jazz band. He had practiced really hard for months. He had been taking lessons all year. He had played well at the tryouts. His friend also tried out for the band.

_____

_____

16.4 The Concluding Sentence   Exercise 120

> Many paragraphs end with a **concluding sentence**. The concluding sentence usually restates the main idea of the paragraph. It also can summarize the information in the paragraph. It usually does not add new information. In the example below, the concluding sentence is underlined.
>
>   Microwave ovens are safe if you use them correctly. Never put metal in the microwave. Use only microwave-safe dishes. Always stop the oven before opening the door. Never turn on the oven when it is empty. <u>Following these rules will keep you safe when using a microwave oven.</u>

Write a concluding sentence for each paragraph below.

1. Do not be scared if you ever see a chuckwalla. It will not hurt you. It is a kind of harmless lizard. Chuckwallas live in the deserts of the United States and Mexico. They eat leaves and flowers. When a chuckwalla sees an enemy, it hides in the crack of a rock.

   _____

2. Many teenagers do chores to earn an allowance. Some help clean the house. Others take out the garbage. Some mow the lawn. Most teenagers clean up their rooms and make their beds.

   _____

CRITICAL THINKING

Read the paragraph below. Explain why the last sentence is *not* a good concluding sentence.

    No one argues that Mount Everest is the highest mountain in the world. However, some people do not agree about how high it is. In the 1800s, the height was measured at 29,002 feet. In 1954, it was measured at 29,028 feet. Several people have climbed to the top of Mount Everest.

_____

_____

_____

Name _____   Date _____

▶ 16.5 Transitional Words   Exercise 121

A **transitional word** connects one idea or sentence to another
in a paragraph. Transitional words help organize the paragraph.
A transitional word that comes at the beginning of a sentence is
followed by a comma. Usually, the word *then* is not followed
by a comma.

Common Transitional Words			
also	first	in addition	next
as a result	for example	in fact	soon
finally	however	later	therefore

Add transitional words to the following paragraphs.

1. Making tacos is easy. _____, brown some ground
   beef. _____ chop some onions, lettuce, and
   tomatoes. _____, grate some cheese.
   _____, heat up your taco shells. Put everything in
   a warmed taco shell and enjoy.

2. Something seemed strange as Jorge walked to his door.
   _____, the porch light, which was always on, was
   turned off. _____, his dog usually barked, but
   Jorge heard nothing today. _____, Jorge opened
   his door very carefully. As he walked through the door, everyone
   inside yelled, "Surprise!"

3. There are several easy ways to exercise every day.
   _____, you can use the stairs instead of an
   elevator. _____, you can walk when you are
   traveling short distances. _____, you can park
   farther away when you shop so that you have to walk across the
   parking lot. These small changes can help you get more exercise.

CRITICAL THINKING

**Write two sentences of your own about what you are going to
do after school today. Use at least one transitional word.**

_____

_____

Name_____   Date_____

> Paragraphs help writers organize their sentences. A good paragraph
> has a topic sentence, supporting details, and a concluding
> sentence. It also has transitional words to connect ideas.
>
> Follow the READ, PLAN, WRITE, and CHECK steps to write a good
> paragraph. The tips below will help you PLAN your writing.
>
> **PLAN**   **Gather your ideas and organize them.**
>
> - The questions in the assignments will help you
>   gather your ideas.
> - Create an outline to organize your ideas.

Complete the writing assignment below.

If you had to pick one age to be for the rest of your life, what age would
you choose? Complete the outline below. Tell what age you would choose,
and why. What are some good things about staying this age? What are
some bad things? Write your ideas in complete sentences.

I. There are some good things about being _____ forever.

   A. _____

   B. _____

II. There are some bad things about being _____ forever.

   A. _____

   B. _____

PUTTING IT ALL TOGETHER

What is the perfect age to be? On a separate sheet of paper, write a
paragraph that tells what age you would like to be. Use the outline
that you have created to help you write your paragraph. Include a
topic sentence, supporting details, and a concluding sentence. Add
transitional words to connect your ideas.